'The downfall of Hagan'

Maynooth Studies in Local History

SERIES EDITOR Raymond Gillespie

This volume is one of six short books published in the Maynooth Studies in Local History series in 2008. Like their predecessors most are drawn from theses presented as part of the MA course in local history at NUI Maynooth. Also like their predecessors they range widely over the local experience in the Irish past from the middle ages into the twentieth century. That local experience is presented in the complex social world of which it is part. These were diverse worlds that need to embrace such differing experiences as the fisheries of Arklow, or the world of books and reading in Loughrea. For yet others their world was constructed through the tensions which resulted in the murder of Major Denis Mahon near Strokestown in 1847. The local experience cannot be a simple chronicling of events relating to an area within administrative or geographically-determined boundaries since understanding the local world presents much more complex challenges for the historian. It is a reconstruction of the socially diverse worlds of poor and rich, from the poor of pre-Famine Tallaght to the more prosperous world of the Church of Ireland in the diocese of Lismore. Reconstructing such diverse local worlds relies on understanding what the people of the different communities that made up the localities of Ireland had in common and what drove them apart. Understanding the assumptions, often unspoken, around which these local societies operated is the key to recreating the world of the Irish past and reconstructing the way in which those who inhabited those worlds lived their daily lives. As such studies like those presented in these short books, together with their predecessors, are at the forefront of Irish historical research and represent some of the most innovative and exciting work being undertaken in Irish history today. They also provide models which others can follow up and adapt in their own studies of the Irish past. In such ways will we understand better the regional diversity of Ireland and the social and cultural basis for that diversity. If they also convey something of the vibrancy and excitement of the world of Irish local history today they will have achieved at least some of their purpose.

Maynooth Studies in Local History: Number 77

'The downfall of Hagan': Sligo Ribbonism in 1842

Jennifer Kelly

FOUR COURTS PRESS

Set in 10pt on 12pt Bembo by
Carrigboy Typesetting Services for
FOUR COURTS PRESS LTD
7 Malpas Street, Dublin 8, Ireland
e-mail: info@fourcourtspress.ie
http://www.fourcourtspress.ie
and in North America for
FOUR COURTS PRESS
c/o ISBS, 920 N.E. 58th Avenue, Suite 300, Portland, OR 97213.

ISBN 978–1–84682–115–8

Printed in England by
Athenaeum Press Ltd, Gateshead, Tyne & Wear.

Contents

Acknowledgments

I would like to thank Prof. Raymond Gillespie for inviting me to contribute to the Maynooth Studies in Local History series and for his kindness and good humour along the way. Professor R.V. Comerford and Dr Maura Cronin provided many helpful comments on earlier drafts of this work, and for this I am extremely grateful. I am also thankful for the assistance of the staff at the following libraries and repositories: John Paul II Library NUIM, Sligo County Library, National Library of Ireland, National Archives of Ireland, the National Archives of the UK, Mary Immaculate College Library, Trinity College Library, Dublin. Thank you to Dr Marie-Louise Legg and Fiona Gallagher for their generosity in providing advice and assistance on maps and illustrations of Sligo town in the nineteenth century. The support of my colleagues in the Department of History at NUI Maynooth is greatly valued. A number of friends and colleagues provided much-appreciated assistance and encouragement along the way, among them Gerard Clarke, Dr Frank Cullen, Ann Donohue, Dr Terence Dooley, Dr Georgina Laragy, Dr Clare O'Neill, Dr Ian Speller. Finally, to my family for their good humour and support, thank you.

1. 'The downfall of Hagan'

On the night of Thursday 31 March 1842, Catherine Hagan of Old Market Street in Sligo, heard two females, accompanied by a mob, singing a ballad entitled 'The downfall of Hagan' as they went through Pound Street in the town. The mob repeatedly cheered when the ballad singers came to that part of the song where they wished Hagan would be bound in Hell, calling out that 'they wished he may'.[1] The two singers were accompanied by another man and a woman who handed the ballad sheets out to the waiting crowd. Catherine Hagan had someone procure one of the sheets for her; she then took the copy of the ballad to the local constabulary and reported the incident. Following her complaint, the provost of Sligo, William Faussett, ordered the constabulary to arrest the ballad singers for a breach of the peace. One of the ballad singers, Martha McLean, and one of the ballad sellers, Martha Kirkwood, were arrested. The other two, James and Catherine McLean, husband and daughter of Martha, absconded.[2]

The reason for Catherine Hagan's distress at this occurrence was that the subject of the ballad was her husband, James Hagan, and she feared that the ballad was exciting the populace against her husband, herself and their family.[3] Hagan had been arrested the previous September and charged with being a member of the Ribbon secret society.[4] He had subsequently given information to the authorities on other members of the society in Sligo and was due to give further information at the Armagh assizes in March 1842 and at the Longford assizes later in the year.[5] James Hagan had been a senior member of the secret society and his information led to the arrest and prosecution of numerous other leading Ribbonmen throughout the country, as well as several local leaders in Sligo town and county. According to Catherine Hagan, 'The downfall of Hagan' was sung 'with the intent of deterring and intimidating the said James Hagan from giving testimony as a witness against the said Ribbonmen at the next assizes for Armagh and Sligo.'[6] The provost, William Faussett, agreed with Catherine Hagan as to the purpose of the ballad, and went on to claim that it was also sung in order to prevent other Ribbonmen, presumably in Sligo town, coming forward to claim immunity in return for information on the Ribbon organization.[7]

That the ballad 'The downfall of Hagan' was so popular in Sligo in early 1842 was not surprising. From September 1841, the Ribbon society had started to fall apart in Sligo town and county due to a number of Ribbonmen there coming forward to give information on the system.[8] As a result, the government and local magistrates had enough information to arrest James Hagan and five other leading members of the secret society in Sligo town and this caused considerable unease among ordinary Ribbon members who feared arrest as a result. Unease turned to panic when the constabulary escorted James Hagan to Dublin in February 1842.[9] It was almost certainly these local fears about the extent of Hagan's betrayal of the system that led to an attempt to defame him around the town through the circulation of the ballad.

Catherine Hagan's complaint was taken seriously by the police in Sligo – they too were aware that the song was particularly potent at that time and were probably in no doubt that the Hagan family would be in danger if the mob took the sentiments of the ballad to heart. The ballad condemned Hagan as a duplicitous traitor and claimed that he purposely swore young innocent men into the Ribbon system in order to augment his own income, knowing that their actions could get them transported:

> It was in the year of '41 he began his wicked plan,
> to swear them in all Partymen, as you may understand
> He thinks to banish all our boys across the raging sea;
> that the 7 plagues of Egypt may attend him night and day.[10]

Hagan had made himself particularly obnoxious both to government and the local Sligo population when it emerged that he had continued to swear men into the Ribbon society after he had been arrested and turned approver, safe in the knowledge that he would not be prosecuted for his Ribbon actions as he was under the protection of the government.[11] Subsequent verses of the ballad went on to acclaim the characters of the young Sligo boys of whom Hagan had taken advantage:

> More power to the Sligo boys! Everywhere they be
> Throughout this Irish nation its now the [sic] bear the sway,
> For conduct and behaviour these young men is well known
> In spite of perjured Hagan they'l [sic] flourish now once more.

> Here's to the boys of Pound-street and thro' Sligo town
> They'r [sic] loyal to their country likewise Queen and crown,
> The [sic] defy perjured Hagan as plain as you may see,
> Long may they live in Sligo town [in] spite of their enemy.[12]

The youth of the 'Sligo boys' was no doubt deliberately played upon by the author of the ballad in order to highlight the extent of Hagan's deviousness and present him as a character who had no regard for the lives of others. This was a common aspect of Ribbon trials throughout the 1830s and 1840s where prosecuting counsel often portrayed the leaders of the Ribbon society as vultures who preyed on young innocent Catholic boys who did not know any better.[13] It seems that this aspect of previous Ribbon trials had been picked up by the composer of the ballad as an aspect of Ribbonism that was likely to whip up the feelings of a crowd against the informer Hagan, while having the secondary purpose of exaggerating the innocence of the Sligo Ribbonmen.

'The downfall of Hagan' was not a seditious ballad; however, this did not mean that it was any less potent in its appeal to the crowd. Maura Murphy's work on ballads in the 19th century shows how ballads castigating an unpopular local figure, such as James Hagan, were as serious a problem for contemporary authorities as songs that contained seditious material because the former had just as much power to cause public disturbance.[14] Unfortunately it is not possible to know whether the composer of 'The downfall of Hagan' was a member of the Ribbon society or simply someone who picked up on the popular anti-Hagan sentiment among the town's population in 1841–2. It may have been that James McLean was the composer of the song, as it was he who brought the manuscript copy of the ballad into the printing offices of John Ring in Sligo in order to have over 200 copies printed. The singers of the ballad were the mother and daughter team of Martha and Catherine McLean. The McLean family stayed in a lodging house in Market Street in Sligo town. It was here that they met Martha Kirkwood who helped James McLean disseminate the ballads through the crowd. Martha was the daughter of an itinerant pedlar man and lodged in the same house as the McLeans.[15] It is likely that the McLeans were an itinerant family also, as Catherine Hagan, who lived in the Market Street area of the town, claimed in her information to police that she did not know the names of the ballad singers but would recognize them if she saw them again.[16] Whatever the circumstances of the ballad's composition, the excitement created by its circulation in Sligo town in March 1842 provides an insight into the hostility of a section of the local population towards a man who, if his own numbers were to be believed, could theoretically have had several thousand men in Co. Sligo arrested.[17]

The Downfall of HAGAN

Come all you loyal young men I hope you will draw near
And of this cruel traitor I'd have you now hewnte.
In praise of those Sligo boys these verses now pend down
Perjured Hagan thought to banish them far from their
    Native home.
It was for to gain a living, this villian did begin ;
For to swear in those young men he thought it no sin,]
He got them taken in Armagh, and likewise Sligo too,
that vengance may atten him all roads that he does go.

It was in the year of '41 he began this wicked plan,
to swear them in all Partymen, as you may understand
He thinks to banish all our boys across the raging sea ,;
that the 7 plagues of Egypt may attend him night & day

Its for the boys of Sligo their equals cant be found,
For modesty and behaviour thro'out this nation round ;
Perjured Hagan thinks to banish then from their native
    Land,
But they have worthy gentlemen, thank God their friend
    to stand.
My curse attend you Hagan wherever you may be;
You got those young men taksn withoutdread or fear,
But they'l be liberated in spite of his perjury;
that satan may embrace him before trial day.

Its for Mr. Fausset his praise I will sound,
thro' ought this Irish nation in country and in town,
he has those young men's blessing all roads he does go
the Lord be his protector and guard his foe.

I s for perjured HAGAN, his name I will tell,
throughout the Irish nation the people knows him well
then for to swear against those boys this villian didnt fail
that — may be his portion upon his dying day

Long Life to Father FEENY and long may he reign,
Likewise the   gentleme ef honor birth and fame,
For to free those Sligo boys they wrought right manfully
Long may theA live in splendor their guardians for to be,

More power to the Sligo boys ! every where they be
throughout this Irish nation its now the bear the sway,
For conduct & behaviour these young men is well known
In spite cf perjured HAGAN they'l flourish now once more

Here's to the boys of Pound-street and thro' Sligo town
they'r loyal to their country likowise the Queen and
    crown,
the defy perjured HAGAN as plain as you may see,
Long may they live in sligo town spite of their enemy,

Now to conclude and finish I have no more to say,
the Lord may guard the sligo boys from danger set them
    free,
As for perjured HAGAN Hagan we'l never see him more,
For he'l be bound in Pluto's chains before he does come
    home.

1. 'The downfall of Hagan'
Source: NAI, CSORP, OR: 10833 26 1842

2. The Ribbon Society in Sligo

The Ribbon secret society was an illegal Catholic sectarian society, formed in the early 19th century in opposition to the Protestant Orange Order. The Ribbonmen originated from previous secret societies, such as the Defenders, who were themselves largely subsumed into the Society of United Irishmen in 1795. For most of the 19th century, Ribbonism was split between two factions, the Ulster and Leinster Ribbonmen. Both factions were organized hierarchically at local, regional, and national level, and both culminated in a ruling board of national delegates. Although the Ribbon society was exclusively Catholic in its membership, it was proscribed by the Catholic Church and the punishment for men suspected of being members of the secret society was excommunication. Besides its sectarian motivations, however, the Ribbon society functioned for its members on a local level almost as a type of mutual assistance society. James Hagan gave his own description of the objectives of the Ribbon society at the Longford assizes in 1842:

> The objects of the society were directly opposed to Orangeism. If any member of the society was dispossessed of his land, and anyone else took it, he would not get long to live. If you annoyed any of the society you would get a good hiding, if you got off with that. In such cases a meeting was called by the parish master, who directed what was to be done to the people giving offence.[1]

At a local level, Ribbonism operated as a parish or district lodge, composed of around 30 or so members, headed by a parish or body master. All were under the control of the county delegate who represented the Ribbonmen in a particular county at the quarterly national delegate meetings.[2]

Although the two Ribbon factions vied for members in all the districts in which they were active, the Ulster faction was more successful in recruiting members in the Sligo region, and references to the Ribbon society in Co. Sligo almost always concerned the Ulster faction.[3] According to a Ribbon informer in 1836, there were six Ribbon lodges in the town of Sligo in 1836, as well as numerous lodges in the surrounding county.[4] The usual meeting place for town lodges was the public house. A lodge met at Christal's public house in Holbourn Street; another met at Michael Connor's on the Mall. Two of the lodges held their meetings in Peter Hart's pub on Knox's Street.[5] One of those lodges was led by Michael Devany, who worked as a ticket clerk for a businessman named James Campbell.[6] A fifth Ribbon lodge was based in 'Loughlin's,' which was most likely a reference to McLaughlin's public house in New Bridge Street.[7] This lodge was headed by a tailor from Cleavragh called McGuire. There was no location given for the sixth lodge, but it was headed by Paddy Morrin who worked in Tempany's grocery store in High Street.[8] By 1842, the number of Ribbon lodges in the town appeared to have increased to ten, each lodge headed by a different body master.[9]

Ribbon lodges in the surrounding countryside are much harder to locate in the sources. However, there is evidence to show that there were Ribbon lodges active in particular places throughout Sligo county. According to an informant in 1836, Ribbonmen in the parish of Drumcliff were allowed to send two parish masters to represent them at the county level meetings because it was such a large parish.[10] In July 1836, two men were arrested in Ganning's public house in Tubbercurry: they were endeavouring to conceal Ribbon passwords at the time of their arrest.[11] In December of the same year, two men with Ribbon passwords were arrested by the police in the house of the Widow Cawly, also in Tubbercurry.[12] In 1839, Ribbon documents were found on Owen Connaughton in Easkey and brought to Sligo to be investigated further. At the same time in Easkey, the house of a man named John Heavy was searched for Ribbon papers.[13] And on the night of 18 July 1840, all of the public houses in Easkey were searched by the Sligo magistrate, John O'Brien, and a party of police. This was done because information had been received that a meeting of Ribbonmen from the surrounding districts would take place in the area on that night.[14] Further information received by the authorities in 1842 indicated that, in addition to Drumcliff, a number of parishes in the county supported two Ribbon parish masters. Among these were the parishes of Coolbeg, Kilmactraney, Riverstown, Ballymote, Dromard, Skreen, Easkey, Kilglass, Kilmacshalgan and Doonaghentra. Some parishes, such as Souey and Templeboy, even supported three parish masters in 1842, while others, namely, Ballyrush and Tannagh, only supported one parish master between them.[15] That so many rural Sligo parishes were either territorially large enough or contained enough Ribbonmen to warrant more than one parish master provides some insight into the sheer spread of one faction of the Ribbon secret society throughout one particular county in the early 19th century.

As with any secret society, precise membership numbers for Ribbonism in Sligo are impossible to quantify. An informant in the 1830s maintained that 'all the Peasantry [sic] between sixteen and fifty years of age were engaged in it.'[16] James Hagan's own evidence also provides some insight into the extent of Ribbon membership in the county. He joined the Ribbon

- ■ Ribbon meeting raided by police, 22 February 1836
- ● Areas where Ribbon lodges were located
- ▲ Ribbon documents discovered at James Hagan's house, Old Market Street, 24 September 1841

OS 1:10,560, Sligo, sheet 14, 1837

2. Locations of Ribbon lodges in Sligo town

society in 1825, and by 1836 he appears to have been quite an influential member of the secret society in Sligo.[17] At that stage, he was master of the Sligo borough, one of the most senior positions in the county apart from that of the county delegate. It was Hagan's responsibility as borough master in the town to swear new members into the secret society, and according to his own evidence, he initiated at least 2,000 men in a six-year period.[18] These numbers, however, may have been slightly inflated, as Hagan was also delegate for part of the county of Longford and his 1842 figures may have included converts to the society from that county as well as some from north Leitrim.[19] R.V. Comerford, in his work on the Fenians of the later 19th century, has highlighted the fact that for a society like the Irish Republican Brotherhood, distinguishing between members and non-members was not always easy.[20] It would appear that Sligo Ribbonmen, by the late 1830s, also had difficulties in distinguishing between the two. According to evidence sworn before William Faussett in March 1839, the society's leadership in Sligo in 1838 decided to undertake an internal audit of active Ribbon members throughout the county. This decision was taken because the county delegate, James Hagan, felt that 'he was not getting in the Dues [sic] regularly.' The count revealed approximately 3,475 men who were part of the secret society throughout the whole county in 1838. As these figures came from the parish masters within the county and were intended for the society's own use, the figures are arguably the most reliable available, at least to the extent that they demonstrate how many members the Ribbon leadership thought they had.[21] On the other hand, it can also be said that local parish masters who may not have been forwarding their dues regularly or accurately, may also not have returned accurate membership numbers for their local lodges. What is significant, however, is that the decision to count the members was taken in order to get 'a return of the number of members they could partly depend on', suggesting that the Sligo Ribbonmen did not, or could not, make the distinction between members and non-members that clearly either.[22]

Previous research on the social profile of the Ribbon secret society in Ireland has shown the cross-class nature of the movement which in many ways reflected the broader contemporary society within which the secret society operated. Men from the trading classes tended to be the leaders of the society, while the rank-and-file was generally composed of the lower social strata.[23] While James Hagan was the borough master for Sligo, a man named Patrick Dunnigan was the Sligo county Ribbon delegate. This was the most senior Ribbon position at county level, and as such, Dunnigan was entitled to attend the ruling board meetings of the Ulster Ribbon faction. Dunnigan was a shopkeeper in Sligo town, a man the authorities regarded as socially much above the station of the average Ribbonman in the town. He was literate and corresponded regularly with the informer James Monaghan.[24]

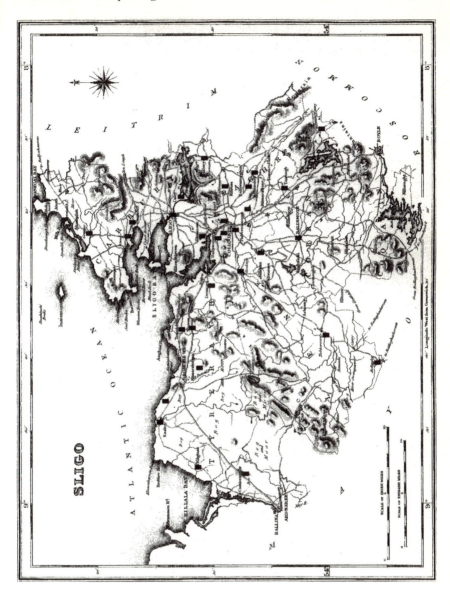

3. Locations of Ribbon lodges in Co. Sligo, 1841.

The contemporary authorities' perception of Dunnigan's social status is significant as the early-19th century authorities usually took comfort from the fact that no man of any social standing appeared to take part in the Ribbon system.[25] Certainly the other Ribbonmen that came to the attention of the Sligo authorities in the 1830s and 1840s appeared to fit the profile of the typical Ribbonman as one who belonged mainly to the small trading and carrying classes. Hagan himself was a journeyman tobacco pipemaker, as was a friend of his, Michael Navin, who also gave evidence against the Ribbonmen in Sligo. The two men had been apprentices together in the 1820s, and both operated pipemaking businesses in Sligo town.[26] A young Sligo Ribbonman named John Coan who was arrested in Dublin in 1836 was a tailor who had, he claimed, travelled to the capital in search of work. He had lived in Armstrong's Row in the town of Sligo and his father was a maltster in Abraham Martin's distillery in the town. Coan admitted being a member of 'Mick' Connor's lodge located on the Mall in Sligo, and at the time of his arrest he was lodging in a back house near Manor Street in Dublin which belonged to a woman named Peggy Murphy.[27] In 1836 the Ribbon informer, James Monaghan, was regarded by the local authorities as being 'much in need of' money and the local sub-inspector of police was authorized to make small payments to him in exchange for information on the leading members of Sligo Ribbonism. In Monaghan's submission to the provost, William Faussett, he claimed his motivation for informing was to 'recover [his] lost sense of social duty', but the letter went on to point out that any prospective information would be supplied on the condition that 'your Hon. [sic] consider me with the smallest recommendation for my small family', indicating that Monaghan did not come from the upper echelons of the town's working classes.[28] The evidence that exists for Ribbon lodge leaders in Sligo town also corroborates the social profile of the Sligo Ribbonmen as coming mainly from the small trading and artisan strata – Michael Devany, leader of the Knox St. lodge, was a ticket clerk, the leader of another lodge in the town was a tailor from Cleaveragh, and a third worked as a storeman in the town.[29] The information given to Sligo magistrates by one informant suggested that men joined the Ribbon society in order to augment low or subsistence incomes. In evidence received by William Faussett in 1836, the informant gave as his reason for joining the Ribbonmen the poor wages that he was receiving in his employment: 'It is a well-known fact to them all that it was the little money I was earning under _____ to serve _____ [sic] that caused me to associate with them'.[30] In the surrounding countryside, the Ribbonmen came mainly from the corresponding labouring and small farming classes, and for these men also joining the Ribbon society was important for their employment prospects, not only at home but also in America. According to James Monaghan in 1836, Sligo labourers travelling to America were anxious to bring the Ribbon passwords with them when they travelled in order to aid them in getting employment at their destination. James Hagan later gave evidence to the same effect in October 1841. According to him, the American lodges issued their own passwords which were in turn transmitted to the Ribbon delegates in Ireland. The Irish delegates then supplied the American and current Irish passwords to the emigrants going to America. Hagan also maintained that the American lodges were so numerous that only 21 men were allowed in each one, and that they were principally connected with the Ulster system of Ribbonism in Ireland.[31]

Of course, it was not simply status that influenced the shape of Ribbonism in 19th century Ireland. There were also intricate levels of internal hier-archies within the Ribbon society itself which often superseded, or worked independently of, a person's social status.[32] This hierarchy stretched from the level of the ordinary lodge member to that of the county delegate the most powerful position within the society. The intervening levels comprised parish masters and body masters; the latter appeared to be the urban equiva-lent of the former, although in some of the sources the terms appear to be interchangeable.[33] In 1841, a Sligo Ribbon informer, Michael McGarry, provided the following information on the organization of the secret society:

> The highest authorities recognized by the body are the county delegates who assembled [sic] at a place and time fixed by the Chairman and a committee on the previous meeting day. These frame the resolutions and passwords for the three subsequent months. They are about 16 [sic] in number with six more from England and Scotland, who attend punctually. Their travelling expenses are defrayed by the officers next in authority called parish masters each paying the delegate five shillings per quarter … These masters he [delegate] assembles on his return home with a view of disclosing to them and thro' them to the members the signs &c. [sic] for the quarter and in the course of a few days instructs the Borough Master in the same.[34]

The links between the parish lodges and the ruling committee of the particular Ribbon faction, in this case the Ulster faction, can be clearly seen from McGarry's evidence. The 'Chairman' alluded to in his evidence is the chairman of the ruling committee of the faction, a position which appeared to alternate between different delegates for a set period of time. Michael McKiernan, the Leitrim county delegate, was chairman of the Ulster faction board for three years during the late 1830s.[35] By 1842, John Rice, the Monaghan county delegate, was chairing the Ulster ruling board.[36] The 'Borough Master' to which McGarry alluded appeared to straddle the divide between parish or body master and county delegate, and as the title implied, applied to the urban borough areas. Borough masters had charge of all of the lodges or bodies existing in a particular borough and so those body masters were subservient to this official. James Hagan was the borough master in the borough of Sligo in the later 1830s and the evidence certainly suggests that his was a more senior position within the society than that of the ordinary body or parish masters.[37] Michael McGarry also provided information to the authorities on the duties of a borough master:

> He (the borough master) assembles his body masters who are ten in number and prepares them to make the same known to the members in the Borough who number 400 or more while those of the county may be said to be 900 – say thirty the average of each parish – the parished being thirty and upwards. The parish meetings are held every month as are those of the borough at which time their respected [sic] masters preside in order to investigate any causes of complaint and to install new members which alone the masters are competent to do with the consent however of their 12 council men in the rural districts and in the borough of the body masters and county delegate. Each member on his initiation pays 2/6 to his master, 1/ for the master, 6d. to the member introducing him, the remainder they pay for drink. Each body master pays 1/ per quarter to the borough master. Each borough [member] 6d. per quarter to the body master and each parish member the same to his parish master for the renewals and a glass of spirits wherewith he may toast prosperity to the body – the balance the master calls his own.[38]

The lines of internal Ribbon authority are easier to trace in the urban context – each lodge or body had a master who was subservient to the borough master who in turn was under the county delegate. In theory, the same applied in the rural context in that the '12 council men' referred to by McGarry replaced the urban body masters. However, these council men of the rural lodges are much harder to trace in the sources and it is unlikely that all rural parish lodges had such clearly defined committee structures.[39]

It is not always clear how some members ascended to the senior positions within the Ribbon society. The sources indicate that there was some form of democratic process involved; certainly the Ribbonmen elected delegates to the committees of their ruling boards, and the delegates also voted on the new passwords every quarter.[40] However, with regard to elevation to the localized senior positions such as parish masters, not all members were eligible for election. Only the literate members of the society could go forward for these positions. Contemporary informers on the Ribbon society were quite explicit on this point – one informer at the Longford assizes in 1842 stating: 'I have very often attended Ribbon meetings and it is at the superior class of them composed of those who can read and write, that the passwords are given for distribution.'The same informant later stated that the 'common illiterate members cannot make Ribbonmen'.[41] All the senior members of the Ulster faction of Ribbonism in the 1830s and 1840s were literate, some of them to quite a sophisticated level, and James Hagan was no exception to this.[42] On two occasions in September 1841, the police discovered copies of the Ribbon passwords hidden in Hagan's house in Market Street; in the first instance, one copy of the passwords was discovered folded up and hidden in a book in a cupboard in the house, while another set was found written down in a book.[43] At the Armagh assizes in 1842, Hagan used a notebook in which he had supposedly recorded his evidence beforehand, to refresh his memory while on the witness stand. This was objected to by the defence counsel but he was nevertheless allowed to go on.[44] During the same trial, Hagan confirmed that he was in regular written communication with other members of the secret society, and that he received letters regularly from other Ribbon delegates. Some of the letters were addressed to himself, and others were addressed to his wife in order to allay suspicion about the amount of correspondence that Hagan received. In some instances the letters arrived to Hagan through the postal system, while others were delivered by hand.[45] It was not unusual for the Ribbonmen to take precautions with their mail during this period. The authorities kept an eye on the number of letters some Ribbon delegates received in the late 1830s, and some were intercepted and copied before being sent on to their destination.[46]

Recent research on the Ribbon society in neighbouring Co. Leitrim has shown that literacy was one of the factors used to preserve the exclusiveness of the leadership groups in the secret society.[47] This was not all that surprising given the often negligible and frequently ill-defined social divisions among the lower strata of the population during this period. Given that money and property, the traditional quantifiers of social respectability in the early 19th century, were not ubiquitous enough to cause significant social division in the society, and political enfranchisement was only becoming available to some leading members of the Ribbon society from 1838 on, literacy was one of the few remaining quantifiable methods of defining social hierarchies within the Ribbon society.[48] In fact it is possible to see in the sources for the Ribbon society, the advancement of literacy even among the lower social strata during this period. By 1839, it appeared that established Ribbon delegates were challenged for their positions by an increasingly literate rank-and-file membership, and additional measures were taken to halt this assault on the privileges of the elite within the society. A document was produced by the ruling committee of the Ulster faction, stipulating that from then on, any man wishing to put himself forward for election in place of another delegate, had to qualify for a property of £100 in order to be eligible.[49] Although it appeared there were other motivations behind this particular document (such as infighting among some of the delegates), it is clear that, from then on, literacy was not enough on its own to make it through the ranks of the society.[50]

Although the exclusive and lucrative senior positions within the Ribbon society were reserved for the privileged few, there appeared to be other divisions, independent of literacy, among the rest of the membership, and this was nowhere more prevalent than in Sligo Ribbonism in the later 1830s and early 1840s. The evidence for Leitrim in the same period suggests that Ribbonism in local parishes was often a method for young men to establish themselves in the social pecking order within their localities, but it is not clear on what basis these divisions were established and maintained.[51] In Sligo, on the other hand, divisions among the Ribbonmen appeared to centre on a combination of levels of membership and something akin to social and economic snobbery. Not all Ribbonmen entered the society on an equal footing. Although the exact nature of membership is difficult to define, it would appear that there were two levels of swearing a member into the secret society. The evidence collected from Sligo by the 1839 house of lords' committee on crime in Ireland referred to two different membership oaths for the Ribbon society. The first contained seven articles which all members swore when first initiated into the society. Among the terms of this 'warrant' were oaths of obedience to the rules of the fraternity as well as loyalty to the 'lawful superiors' of the society. There was also a stress on the importance of regular attendance at Ribbon meetings, presumably in order to maintain the income of the society's officers. References in the oath to aiding fellow members in distress reflected the broader mutuality aspects of Ribbonism – in this respect 'distress' covered economic hardship as well as a promise to fight in defence of a fellow member. The importance of maintaining preferential dealings among fellow members or the wider Catholic trading community was also a feature of the basic Ribbon oath.[52] This oath was almost identical to one given by a Leitrim Ribbonman to a magistrate in Mohill in that county in 1840 and it is most likely that this was the form of the oath used by Ribbonmen throughout the Ulster faction during the later 1830s.[53]

However, the Sligo informant that supplied this oath to William Faussett in 1836 claimed in an accompanying letter that the men sworn to the seven articles were not admitted into the 'regular body' of the Ribbon society, and that 'the Persons [sic] who are properly made are sworn to the Fourteen Articles,' indicating a further level of membership within the society's structure.[54] A copy of the 14 articles which this informant was referring to had been seized by Faussett and the police in a raid on a Ribbon meeting in Sligo in February 1836. The document was found in a chest in the house of a leading Ribbonman in the town, most likely Patrick Dunnigan, the county delegate for Sligo prior to Hagan's takeover. The 14 articles in many respects were simply a more detailed version of the initial seven, but they also contained some additional important clauses that may only have been applicable to the more senior members of the society. As Faussett's informant pointed out in 1836, the 14 articles were used by the 'regular' body of Ribbonmen, and it is clear when comparing the two forms of the Ribbon oath that the second requires more in terms of membership than the first. In fact, when the Ribbonmen referred to 'regular' members, they were not referring to the whole body of sworn Ribbonmen in a particular area; rather they were alluding to the men that formed the electable or enfranchised part of the society, in other words, those that would go on for election to the senior positions within the society. References within the 14 articles specifically alluded to the senior committee meetings of the Ribbonmen and one of the clauses of the oath implied that only men who attended the local or national committee meetings of the Ribbon faction were required to take this oath, 'That I will never discover of any of my true and loyal B[rethre]n ... or anyone here present'. This was further backed up by another article in the warrant which alluded to the payment of a fine in the event of non-attendance at these meetings. Since men in these positions within the society were privy to more information on the structures and senior personnel of Ribbonism it was vital that they remain loyal to their brethren under all conditions. This was reflected strongly throughout the 14 articles with three separate sections referring to informing on fellow members. One of the terms of the oath, which prohibited excessive drunkenness at meetings of Ribbonmen in order to guard against naming individuals who were senior men in the society, may even indicate that the senior members were not always known to members below them in the society's ranks and that this distance may have been deliberately cultivated.[55] This was also evident in separate evidence given before the sub-inspector in Sligo, William Tracy, where the informant in question was unable to name any more senior members than the delegate for his county, indicating that knowledge of the members of the senior committee of the Ulster faction of Ribbonmen did not travel very far down the Ribbonite hierarchy.[56]

Other strongly stressed aspects of the 14 articles were preference in trade dealings among fellow members or other Roman Catholics, and the onus on members to attend promptly when called upon by fellow members. The Ribbon mutuality system was obvious in the seventh article which advocated relieving fellow members with money, lodgings or food when required. Senior members of the Ribbon society used this system of reciprocity when travelling to delegate meetings throughout Ireland and Britain.[57] This aspect of Ribbonism very much reflected the contemporary tramping system prevalent among tradesmen in Ireland and England in the 19th century. Interestingly, the oath also extended the mutual support system of Ribbonism to members' families; this was an aspect of Ribbonism which was also carried on by the Leinster faction where money from that society's funds was given to members' families for sundry purposes.[58] The fourth term of the 'regular' oath, not to fight against fellow members, also contained provision for advising them when they might have been in the wrong: 'but if a B[rothe]r be in fault I will advise and save him if possible I can do so.'[59] It is possible that this feature of the oath was intended to protect against intra-Ribbon dissent at the senior meetings, where members sometimes argued against each other as to the interpretation of the rules of the society. Certainly these kinds of intra-delegate disputes and their resolution constituted the main business of an Ulster faction delegate meeting held in Ballinamore in Co. Leitrim in 1840.[60] All in all, the security features against informers and the stress on loyalty and brotherhood throughout the 14 articles suggests that the men swearing this oath were of a higher standing in the secret society than those who were simply required to swear the oath containing seven articles.

However, there appeared to be further divisions in status among Sligo Ribbonmen in this period, even among the group of members who may not have been eligible for election to the higher ranks of the society. The lowest membership level within Sligo Ribbonism appeared to be that of the three-penny-men. According to the informant James Monaghan, these men, who were 'in the habit of waylaying and beating,' were not admitted into the regular Ribbon society, but used almost as an auxiliary force of 'heavies' to enforce local Ribbon policy in the community.[61] Although it is not clear what exactly separated the three-penny-men from the ordinary Ribbonmen, it may be that the name referred to the amount that these men paid to be affiliated to the Ribbon society, 3d. If this was the case, then it suggests that the three-penny-men were economically less well-off than the ordinary Ribbon members, indicating that at least some of the internal divisions in Ribbonism were based on social or economic status. An informant at a trial of Ribbonmen at the Longford assizes in 1840 testified that the prices he paid for the Ribbon passwords varied from 2d. to 2½ d. All the men indicted in his evidence were farmers' labourers.[62] Other Ribbonmen in Longford, however, paid 6d. for their passwords during the same period.[63] In Leitrim also, there was evidence that some Ribbonmen paid less than the going rate for their passwords. William McPadden and Patrick McPartland, both labourers in the parish of Drumreilly in south Leitrim, paid 3d. each on their entry to the local Ribbon lodge in that part of the country. Although this evidence can be taken to suggest that perhaps the Ribbon society tailored its costs to suit the economic means of local communities in pre-Famine Ireland, it is perhaps more likely that the men who paid these prices for their passwords were not initiated into the regular body of Ribbonmen, but merely existed as a fighting reserve for the secret society.[64] It is also likely that the reason that these men had a particular title in Sligo town in the late

1830s and were not identified as separate to the main Ribbon body in more rural areas, was because the Ribbon hierarchical system was less obviously structured in the rural areas than in the urban centres.

There is other tentative evidence throughout the sources for Ribbonism in Sligo and elsewhere that suggest that a lower level of Ribbonman, possibly the three-penny-men referred to by the informer Monaghan, operated as the physical force element of Ribbonism. In June 1836, following Patrick Dunnigan's resignation from the position of Ribbon county delegate for Sligo, information received by the Sligo authorities indicated that there was a certain amount of intrigue among the senior Sligo Ribbonmen as to who would succeed Dunnigan as county delegate.[65] In one informant's letter it was stated that one of those contending for the county delegate's position brought men to act as 'bullies' for him at one particular Ribbon meeting in the town, 'very likely he will have ____, and one ____ from this St., a ____ Man, with him, as Bullys, because ____ of ____ ____ and ____ are contending for the Chieftainship of the Co. [sic] at large'.[66] The implication here is that the various applicants for the senior Ribbon position had their own factions to support them, and it is tempting to assume that the '____ Man' referred to in the quotation above was a three-penny man. Certainly other senior Ribbon members in pre-Famine Ireland seemed to have had their own factions who were called on when extra numbers were needed for a certain purpose.

Michael McKiernan and Farrell Kiernan, two of the leading members of the Ulster faction of Ribbonism in neighbouring Co. Leitrim, assembled a faction to fight against an opponent from Cavan in order to settle an old score at the Ballinamore fair in 1842. At least 400 men were involved on each side and the battle had taken many months to organize. Large numbers of the men came from Fermanagh as well as Cavan and Leitrim.[67] McKiernan had previously been involved in a dispute in 1839 with Michael O'Neal, the Longford delegate of the Leinster Ribbonmen, in which factions were also used to back each side up.[68] Although there is no conclusive evidence that the men involved in these particular factions were three-penny men or of some other equivalent status, it is likely that some of the almost 800 men involved in the 1842 affray were only tangentially affiliated to the formal Ribbon system.

There is other evidence to suggest that men who were not members of the Ribbon society sometimes took part in Ribbonite activities in the early 19th century. Information from Ribbon informants in other areas implied that not all the men involved in large-scale Ribbon activities were regular members of the society, and undoubtedly some of them were drafted in to augment numbers on particular occasions. Thomas Meehan, a weaver from Kilmore in Co. Leitrim gave evidence to the police in 1839 on the activities of a Ribbon lodge in Derry Lagham in Co. Cavan. Although the reasons for

Meehan providing information to the police on Ribbonism were dubious at best, the contemporary authorities did admit that facets of it were corroborated by external independent sources indicating that Meehan was somewhat familiar with the Ribbon system in Cavan. In his evidence, Meehan provided information on a system of intimidation carried out at the instigation of the local Ribbon lodge on two Leitrim men who took land in Derry Lagham. According to his evidence, a meeting of over 100 men took place in a field in Derry Lagham in 1834 at which the decision to banish the Leitrim men from the area was taken. At this meeting, the parish masters present informed all of the men there 'that it was a dangerous business they were engaged in, that any person who acted contrary to his oath would be shot.' The parish masters also swore the men 'to be loyal and true, to back each other on all occasions until the Derrylagham [sic] affair should be ended, not to give any information or speak of any person or thing they might hear or see during the night'.[69] The intimidation and the phrasing of this particular oath suggested that not all the men present that night were regular members of the Ribbon society and as such could not be trusted to stick together. Also the length of time covered by the oath, i.e. 'until the Derrylagham affair should be ended', further suggests that extra men, who were perhaps not Ribbonmen, were sworn in to augment the numbers of the party.[70] It is possible that some of these men were what would have been regarded in Sligo at the time as 'three-penny men.'

Although the Cavan evidence indicated that not all the men who took part in the Ribbon attack on Derry Lagham were members of a Ribbon lodge, there is other evidence to show that Ribbonmen could also become involved in outrages in their own or neighbouring localities which were not necessarily Ribbon attacks. Terence Dooley's perceptive exploration of the Wildgoose Lodge atrocities of 1816 in Co. Louth has shown how overlapping membership of the Ribbon secret society and of local agrarian factions in pre-Famine Ireland sometimes fed into general agrarian discontent at a popular level.[71] In many respects, it can be argued that the three-penny members of the Ribbon society often blurred the lines of distinction between the secret society and loosely-organized and ill-defined local agrarian gangs. Thomas Meehan in Cavan also provided further evidence on how men were gathered to beat a Sligo Protestant at the Ballyshannon harvest fair in 1837, which suggested that men who were not regular Ribbon members were incorporated into the attacking party and also demonstrated how easily the Sligo Ribbonmen could extend their operations into neighbouring counties. According to Meehan, he had been drinking with two friends from Leitrim at the Co. Donegal fair when he was approached by another Leitrim man who enquired of him if he knew any men in the pub who were 'loyal and true,' and that word had come from Sligo that a man named Allen was to be beaten at the fair for voting against the Catholic candidate at the Sligo election that year. A number of men were gathered at the pub and between them they beat the unfortunate Allen when he was pointed out to them by the Leitrim Ribbonman.[72] Meehan did not know all the men who made up Allen's attacking party and the way in which the men were gathered for the activity, by enquiring around a pub as to who was loyal, indicated a much broader affiliation with the Ribbon society which incorporated more than the regular Ribbon society's formal lodge members.

Meehan's evidence also indicated indirectly how involved the Ribbonmen were in the intimidation surrounding the 1837 election in Sligo town and suggests that though formal Ribbon objectives tended to concentrate on mutuality among members, rank-and-file Ribbonmen were often involved in other popular agitations in the county. The 1837 Sligo borough election appeared to inflame sectarian feelings in the county at a popular level. This was primarily because the Liberal candidate, John Martin, had fallen out of favour with the local Catholic clergy, because he was perceived as having abandoned his liberal principles and aligned himself with the Tories. Despite Martin's protestations against these accusations, Sligo Liberals chose another candidate to represent them in the borough election of 1837. The Catholic Administrator of Sligo, the Revd James Donlevy, and the bishop of Elphin, Patrick Burke, both strongly supported the alternative liberal candidate, John Somers, and enthusiastic rallies were held in the town in July of that year. The election took place over a three-day period, 2 to 5 August, and Somers emerged victorious.[73] The repercussions of the election results continued at a popular level in the county into the autumn of 1837. On the night of 22 August at Geevagh, a number of bonfires were lit on the local mountain and crowds gathered around them shouting. The reason for the celebrations, according to the local constabulary, was a report that was circulated claiming that a prominent Sligo landholder, Colonel Perceival, had been struck dead as a result of a curse imposed on him by a priest at the Sligo election. Perceival had supported the candidacy of Martin in the election and the priest referred to in the report was the pro-Somers Revd James Donlevy. The commotion caused by this report in Geevagh was serious enough for many local Protestant families to leave their homes on that night fearing attack by the crowds surrounding the bonfires.[74]

On the other hand, it appeared that some men existed on the fringes of Sligo Ribbonism, independent of the three-penny-men and without engaging in any of the society's activities. It was certainly possible to be affiliated to the Ribbon system through trading channels in pre-Famine Ireland without actually being a member of the secret society. The information received by William Faussett in Sligo in 1836 referred on numerous occasions to the need for Catholic petty tradesmen to have access to the relevant Ribbon passwords for the purposes of carrying on their businesses.

One informant wrote to him in January 1838 claiming that it was dangerous for people in his 'rank of life' not to become Ribbon members as 'he [sic] has just reason to believe that there are Persons employed for Payment to beat or otherwise ill-treat Persons who are not Members'.[75] Although this man did not state what his rank was, he was most likely a petty tradesman in Sligo town. Faussett gave his own opinion to the 1839 enquiry into crime in Ireland that 'those Persons who go to Fairs and Markets are obliged to become Members of that Body to insure their safety.'[76] Thomas Meehan, the Leitrim informant mentioned above, was a weaver who travelled for his trade. He informed the police in Leitrim about another Ribbon meeting that took place in Cavan in 1834 where it was decided that tradesmen in the locality that did not belong to the Ribbon society should be targeted and 'that it would be well to give them a warning.' As a result of that meeting, several tradesmen in the locality were visited by the Ribbonmen and beaten because they were regarded as being adverse to the Ribbon system.[77] Undoubtedly Meehan's work as a weaver was one of the main reasons for his joining the Ribbon society in that part of the country.

Carmen were also targeted by the Ribbonmen as they travelled around to fairs and markets in different counties or even in some cases across the country, from Sligo to Dublin. It was important for these men to know the correct answers to questions put to them by the Ribbonmen when they were stopped, if their goods were to be protected.[78] This was one of the ways in which the Ribbon society perpetuated its monopoly on some aspects of petty trading among the lower commercial strata in pre-Famine Ireland. Four men were indicted in the Sligo courts in March 1836 for stopping and attacking a carman who was returning from a fair in Ballisodare when he was unable to answer correctly what were clearly Ribbon questions. The carman was beaten severely and his horse attacked as a result of his inability to provide the Ribbon passwords for that quarter.[79] Other tradesmen, however, did not have to become members of the society, but it was in their interest to purchase the passwords in any given quarter in order to be allowed to conduct their business without interference from the local Ribbonmen, or in some cases, in order to augment their customer base. Patrick McDonald, the Cavan county delegate for the Ulster faction, regularly sold the Ribbon passwords to P.W. Byrne, an extensive emigration broker, in order to ensure that the latter's business would benefit 'in the getting of passengers from Ireland to give preference to his conveyances.'[80]

In 1842, the Sligo tobacco pipemaker, Michael Navin, gave evidence at the Sligo assizes that he also purchased the Ribbon passwords in Sligo although he was not a sworn member of the Ribbon society. According to his evidence, he got the passwords in order to protect himself as he travelled to fairs and markets throughout the countryside. Navin had been buying the passwords from the then county delegate, James Hagan, who appeared to be a personal friend of Navin's. Hagan had joined the Ribbon society in 1825, and Navin had commenced buying the passwords from him in 1828.[81] Men such as P.W. Byrne and Michael Navin bought the Ribbon passwords to facilitate their respective businesses in the pre-Famine period. However, though not sworn members of the society, it is unlikely that these two tradesmen and others like them, were on the same inferior level as the three-penny men referred to above. Both of them appeared to have viable businesses during the period and in any case, their friendships with two senior members of the society, the Sligo and Cavan county delegates, implies that they were above the three-penny rank and file in Sligo. On the other hand, the weaver, Thomas Meehan, referred to above, appeared to be in a different economic category – he was a travelling weaver who appeared to owe a number of people quite a bit of money and he had previously spent some time in jail. In fact the implication in the source is that it was because some of his creditors were pressing him for the amounts due to them that he decided to prosecute a number of them for such things as assault, riot and unlawful swearing. Incidentally, this was also the reason that the authorities could not use his information on Ribbonism to their advantage.[82] Meehan's uncertain economic circumstances and his position on the fringes of the Ribbon society in pre-Famine Cavan suggests that he was in the category of three-penny men, or at the very least not a member of the regular Ribbon society. He also did not have the wealth of either Byrne or Navin to enable him to perhaps deal with the Ribbonmen from arm's length as they appeared to have done.

However, this ability to deal with the Ribbonmen from a certain social distance only went so far, and in any case, only appeared to extend as far as did the social gap between the two parties. In other words, people like Michael Navin could afford to purchase the Ribbon passwords for their own economic benefit so long as their actions complemented the Ribbon system in their localities (in this case through trading and friendship links), but once the activities of such men as Navin got in the way of the Ribbonmen, retribution could be swift and relatively severe. This was the case in 1841–2 when Michael Navin was apprehended by the police in Sligo and turned informer against the Sligo Ribbonmen.[83] Navin first gave evidence in front of John O'Brien, Esq. on 8 September 1841.[84] However, his information did not appear to be publicly used until the 1842 Sligo July assizes when he gave evidence at the trial of a Ribbonman named Thomas Graham.[85] Within a month, the Ribbonmen in Sligo targeted Navin's pipemaking business in response to his informing. Two men who had purchased pipes from Navin were attacked separately by the Ribbonmen as they were leaving the town with their goods. In one case, a man named Barley Doogan had all his pipes seized. The reason given by the constabulary in their report was that the outrage took place because he had purchased the goods from 'Navin an informer against Ribbonmen'.[87] Later that evening another man, John Cawly, was also attacked on the outskirts of the town as he was carrying away goods which he had purchased earlier. He was overtaken by a gang of seven men, two of whom enquired as to who he had purchased his pipes from. On ascertaining that the pipes were manufactured by Michael Navin, the men forced them from Cawly and broke them up on the road with large stones, warning the victim 'that if he knew anything of Navin they would serve him in like manner'.[87]

In many ways, Michael Navin was very lucky that the Ribbonmen's ire against him only extended to his business dealings in the town, although this in itself could have serious repercussions for his ability to maintain his position locally as a petty trader. In other cases, Sligo tradesmen were not so lucky. A Protestant Scotsman named Symes was targeted by the Ribbonmen in Sligo during the 1830s after he purchased a grain mill at Collooney from a Catholic who had gotten into difficulties with his mortgage on the property.[88] As a result of the Ribbon hold on local petty trading and travelling to markets and suppliers, and because of local sectarian antagonism to Symes, he was unable to carry on his business in Collooney and was forced to sell it back to the original Catholic owner. Once he had done this, his corn business in other parts of the county was allowed to proceed uninterrupted. However, while hostility in Collooney was ongoing against him, carmen from Sligo, Leitrim and Roscommon refused to carry provisions to or from his business because of fear of Ribbon retaliation against themselves or their families, indicating once again, the extent of Ribbon penetration among the lower trading and carrying classes throughout the countryside.[89] Even though James Hagan was himself losing his hold to some extent on the Ribbon system in the town by the time Michael Navin had given his evidence in court, the latter's friendship with the beleagured county delegate, and Navin's Catholicism, may have in some respects saved Navin from the fate of Symes.

3. James Hagan: Sligo Ribbonman

Acting on information from an unnamed source, the provost of Sligo, William Faussett, accompanied by the Constabulary, visited a house on Barrack Hill in the town on 22 February 1836. The house belonged to an elderly man named James Monaghan who was a petty schoolmaster. A Ribbon meeting was taking place in the house at the time of the Constabulary's visit and the eight men present were all arrested. Documents and passwords were found in Monaghan's vest and he confessed to having been a Ribbonman for the previous 30 years.[1] Although Monaghan may have been exaggerating the length of his involvement in the Ribbon society, his evidence does suggest that formal Ribbonism may have existed in Sligo as early as 1806. Even though the link is quite tentative, it is the earliest reference to the organized Ribbon system to date.[2] Although the authorities were not aware of it at the time of the arrests, they had in Monaghan quite an important figure in Sligo Ribbonism. According to his own later evidence, James Monaghan was secretary to Patrick Dunnigan, who was the Sligo county delegate up to 1836, and because of his position, he was privy to a great deal of the organizational information on the workings of the secret society, all of which he appeared to be happy to relate to the authorities in return for immunity from prosecution and a monetary inducement.[3]

Following an initial examination before the town's magistrates, Monaghan and the other men arrested with him were released on bail to appear at the next assizes.[4] In the meantime, Monaghan and another man arrested at the same meeting, Michael O'Hagan, offered to become approvers in return for indemnity from prosecution. William Faussett agreed to provide Monaghan with immunity, most likely because Monaghan would have had more information to provide on the secret society's activities than the others, because of his position as secretary to the county delegate.[5] Monaghan's decision to become approver was an intelligent one, given that the evidence found by the police at the meeting in his house would have convicted only him and not the others present; the government authorities were not entirely happy that Monaghan had been granted immunity for this reason. As it stood after that, they did not have enough evidence to bring any of the other men forward for trial, and so from then on, were dependant on the information provided by Monaghan to indict Ribbonmen in the town at future trials.[6] Monaghan agreed to meet with Faussett and the Constabulary sub-inspector, William Tracy, in a private room at McBride's hotel in the town where he assured them that he would provide them with information on all the principal characters involved in Ribbonism in Sligo town.[7] Monaghan's choice of McBride's hotel as the venue for his meeting with the town's authorities was wise. McBride's, also known as the Lord Nelson hotel, was owned by Robert McBride, a future lord mayor of Sligo and a freemason. The hotel contained the town's grand jury room and it was also the location for the local freemasonry lodge.[8] As such, McBride's was socially distant enough from the types of premises favoured by the Ribbonmen for Monaghan to be confident that he might not be noticed by his Ribbon brethren meeting with Faussett. At this meeting, and in a later series of letters between Monaghan and Faussett, the former identified the county delegate of the Ribbon society in Sligo as Patrick Dunnigan, a shopkeeper in the town, and James Hagan as the borough master of the town.[9] This was the first time that James Hagan was mentioned in the reports on Ribbonism in Sligo and, from informers' reports on the secret society in Sligo town, it is possible to trace Hagan's progression through the Ribbon society from the later 1820s.

James Hagan joined the Ribbon society in 1825 and by 1836 he was the borough master for Sligo town.[10] Along with his tobacco pipe making trade, he also ran a 'provision shop' in Market Street and membership of the Ribbon society, with its system of preferential dealing among members, would have helped him to carry on his business around the vicinity of Sligo's markets and those of neighbouring counties.[11] After the arrest of Monaghan in 1836, Patrick Dunnigan resigned from his position as county delegate in the society.[12] Dunnigan's position as a relatively prosperous shopkeeper in the town in the 1830s, much above the social status of the average Ribbonman, may have been the reason for his immediate departure from the society once Monaghan's information got out. Other leading members in the society, such as James Hagan, did not leave their respective positions after Monaghan informed. Following Dunnigan's secession, there appeared to be some amount of intrigue among the remaining senior members of the society as to who should accede to the position of county delegate. According to Monaghan's evidence, a man named Michael Tighe, from Pound Street, was chosen as successor to Dunnigan. However, a number of members were not happy with this decision, and Tighe was challenged for the delegate's position by another faction within the senior membership group, led by Martin Leadon and James Hagan. A second meeting was held as a result of this dissatisfaction, but the situation did not appear to have been resolved. At the next meeting for disseminating the new quarterly passwords, a three-hour meeting comprised of around ten parish masters was held at Tighe's house in Pound Street, while a separate meeting was held at Hagan's in Market Street, indicating that the disagreement had not yet been settled. Another meeting to discuss the delegate's position was held in Devrey's public house on Knox Street on 14 April 1836; this was the meeting where James Hagan took over as the Sligo county delegate for the Ulster Ribbon faction.[13]

As a Ribbon county delegate, Hagan's duties were much increased in scope from what they had been in his prior position as borough master of Sligo town. He was now responsible for voting on the new quarterly passwords, which were then passed down from him to the parish masters under his control. In 1841, after attending a meeting in Derrynoose, Co. Armagh, Hagan made out 56 copies of the passwords for that quarter, which gives an insight into the number of parishes and lodges under his control at that time.[14] In fact, it was the written copies of the passwords kept in his house in Sligo that provided some of the main evidence against him after his arrest.[15] He was also, from 1836 on, in charge of communications between Sligo Ribbonmen and the ruling committee of the Ulster Ribbon faction. It was his responsibility to attend the quarterly meetings of the Ulster faction and, according to his later evidence, he attended meetings of the faction in places as far apart as Fermanagh, Leitrim, Monaghan and Armagh over a five-year period from 1837 to 1841. Hagan also maintained that he attended a ruling delegate meeting of the Ulster faction in Dundalk in 1834. This was before he had acceded to the position of county delegate for Sligo. This suggests that the Ribbon county delegates could send other representatives to delegate meetings if they could not go themselves. As borough master of Sligo in the early 1830s, Hagan was the obvious choice to send to a delegate meeting in place of Dunnigan if the need arose. In fact Hagan himself sent his borough master, Daniel Fitzpatrick, as the Sligo representative to a delegate meeting that was held in Middletown, Co. Armagh in 1841.

Although the quality and credibility of the information later provided by Hagan to the authorities was generally creditable, it was not without its problems. Hagan's evidence was not always consistent as to the details of the delegate meetings. He provided two different dates for the Enniskillen delegate meeting – in his information to the magistrate, he cited 1837 as the year that the delegates met in the Co. Fermanagh town, but in later evidence at the trials of other leading Ribbonmen in Armagh, he was reported as claiming the Enniskillen meeting took place in 1838.[16] The defence counsel did not question him on this difference in his accounts, which may indicate that the newspaper report was inaccurate in this respect. He also provided two different days for the timing of the Armagh delegate meeting in 1841, which took place at Derrynoose, claiming in one source that it was held on Christmas Day, and in another that it took place on 26 December. In this case, the differing days may have been due to the meeting continuing over a number of days, or to the vagueness of the timing of Ribbon delegate meetings, which were often not specified too closely in order to protect

against informers, particularly after 1840.[17] However, Hagan did appear to be
prone to exaggeration when giving his evidence to the authorities. He
maintained that foreign delegates attended the Enniskillen meeting in 1837
and even hinted that this was not necessarily an uncommon occurrence:
'Delegates occasionally attend from America, saw a delegate attend from
France, George Venoe – the meeting was at Enniskillen, there was scarcely a
delegate from Ireland about on that day'.[18]

Hagan did not appear to have attended all the delegate meetings of
the Ulster faction during his period as county delegate of the Sligo
Ribbonmen, or at least he did not give information on all the meetings to
the Sligo authorities. He attended a meeting in Enniskillen in 1838. There is
no evidence that he attended any of the delegate meetings in 1839. In 1840,
he was present at delegate meetings in Monaghan and in Annayalla, and in
1841, he sent a representative to the Middletown meeting, and attended
himself at a meeting in Derrynoose on or around Christmas Day.[19] He did
not mention attending a delegate meeting that took place in Ballinamore in
neighbouring Co. Leitrim on 9 June 1840 – this was significant because the
authorities had managed to infiltrate this meeting and at least three of the
leading members of the Ulster faction were arrested as a result of the
undercover operation. Two of those three, the Cavan and Tyrone delegates,
were transported.[20] The third senior member, the Leitrim delegate, was
jailed for two years.[21] Although there were 12 Ribbonmen in all arrested at
Ballinamore in 1840, a number of the more important delegates had
managed to elude arrest by either not arriving in time for the meeting or
escaping before the police caught them.[22] Some time after this, a police
informant in Liverpool maintained that the delegates who still remained at
large were all the more dangerous for that: 'they only remain for election
and being sufficiently daring and wary enough to avoid a trap such as the
others fell into [sic] are leaders more to be dreaded'.[23] James Hagan, as
delegate for Sligo and part of Longford, was possibly one of the men to
whom this informant referred.

The evidence that exists for Hagan's involvement in the Ribbon society
after the Ballinamore arrests in 1841 suggests that his was one of the more
prominent delegate positions in the Ulster faction. Following the arrests in
Leitrim, the senior members of the Ulster faction were more than ever
aware of the danger of internal informers – they knew that the authorities
could not have infiltrated the Ballinamore meeting without the help of
insiders. Some of the delegates even started turning on each other, accusing
comrades who had evaded arrest of providing information to the
authorities.[24] The Ulster Ribbon system was very shaken by the infiltration
of the authorities in Co. Leitrim in 1840, and as a result the ruling board of
the faction became even more secretive when meeting to decide on the new
passwords. From July 1840 onwards, only a 'Select' comprised of those

delegates 'who have for a long time been known and respected' were permitted to know of, or attend, the meetings of the ruling board where the new passwords were decided on. These men swore a special oath pledging them to keep the locations of any subsequent delegate meetings a strict secret. This pattern was repeated at regional level by other members of the secret society, in an effort to curtail the possibility of the authorities sending in another infiltrator.[25] James Hagan was one of the delegates entrusted with membership of this exclusive group among the Ribbon leaders, a fact which reflected his importance in the Ribbon organization at a much wider level. As a member of this select group of senior delegates, Hagan attended the Ribbon delegate meetings which followed the Co. Leitrim exposure of the secret society, when the organization was at its most guarded. These meetings took place at Monaghan town on 3 April 1841 and Annayalla, Co. Monaghan, on 3 July in the same year.[26] Hagan was also the delegate chosen to communicate with the Ribbon lodges in Scotland after 1840.[27] This, along with the power to communicate on behalf of the Ulster faction with Ribbon lodges in England, was a particular privilege within the society's hierarchy, and a position which had been jealously guarded by its previous occupier, Patrick McDonald, the Cavan county delegate who had been arrested in 1840.[28] The fact that James Hagan assumed this communication role after 1840 suggests that his was a relatively powerful position even within the select group of leaders who took over control of the Ulster faction after the Ballinamore fiasco.

There is also other evidence which suggests that Hagan's position within the Ulster faction of the Ribbon secret society was a significant one. One of the outcomes of the ill-fated Leitrim delegate meeting was the breaking away of a smaller faction within the Ulster Ribbonmen, who called themselves the Carrick faction. This split occurred because of internal Ribbon suspicions over informers within their ranks. The Carrick faction was primarily composed of Ribbonmen who had been arrested in Ballinamore in June 1840 and their supporters, who came mainly from counties Leitrim, Roscommon and Sligo, and who, according to Hagan's information in 1842, were determined to break away from the Ulster system because 'there were traitors amongst [sic] them – that they would act for themselves [sic] and would apply for the power and protection of France and French arms.'[29] Although James Hagan did not appear to be part of the Carrick faction, he was the man who provided contact between the breakaway faction and the Ulster faction once the split occurred, ironically indicating that he was considered a trustworthy member by both sides in the split. However, it is likely that Hagan was more involved in the Carrick faction than he admitted to either his fellow Ulster faction members or to the investigating magistrates, and perhaps even that the Carrick splinter group had been planning to secede from the Ulster faction's leadership prior to the

Ballinamore arrests. Information received by the government from a Liverpool informant as early as the winter of 1839 located the Carrick splinter group right on Hagan's doorstep: 'There is a body of Ribbonmen in Connaught, distinct from the northern and Dublin societies, and having their headquarters at Sligo.'[30] This information dates the formation of the faction to at least six months prior to the Ballinamore arrests, which were supposedly the motive for seceding in the first place. Incidentally, the members of the Carrick faction were particularly successful at evading police surveillance on their activities in Co. Sligo at a time when other centres of Ribbonism were being infiltrated by police informers. An anonymous letter received by the Sligo magistrate, John O'Brien, in July 1840, maintained that the Carrick faction was meeting in Easkey, Co. Sligo in that month, while the summer assizes were taking place in Sligo town, confident in the knowledge that the local constabulary were going from Easkey to Sligo to attend at the courts. The magistrate and the police proceeded to search all of the public houses in the village of Easkey on the night in question, but no Ribbonmen were discovered on any of the premises. According to the magistrate's report, the faction were alarmed at the proceedings at the Ballinamore trials, which had taken place earlier in July 1840, and so called off their meeting, afraid of drawing attention to themselves. However, it is more likely that fear of an informer in their ranks was the cause of the meeting not taking place, as not only were there no Ribbonmen in any of the pubs searched by the police in the village, 'but the Sub Inspector and Constables [sic] stated that they had never recollected seeing the public houses empty on a Saturday night before'.[31] Clearly, the Ribbonmen in Easkey were proving a point to the local constabulary on this occasion.

Overall then, by the summer of 1840, James Hagan occupied a powerful position within the Ulster faction of Ribbonism – he had at least 56 lodges in counties Sligo and Longford under his command, he also had control of communications links between the Ulster faction and the Scottish lodges, and he was a member of the new select ruling group of the Ulster faction. So when the Sligo authorities breached the secrecy of the Ribbon society in the town for a second time, in 1841, they managed to capture in Hagan one of the most important men still at large in the Ulster faction. For the second time in five years, a series of informers in Sligo provided information on the workings of the system in the town and, in the process, exposed James Hagan. The difference in 1841, however, was that the authorities did not repeat the mistakes of 1836: no immunity was granted to the initial informers, and they made sure that enough evidence was collected to ensure trials would take place. They were helped in this by the fact that both the Leinster and Ulster Ribbon factions had been badly exposed in 1839 and 1840 respectively so, by 1841, the Sligo authorities knew what they could and must get from Hagan to secure convictions for the other leading members of the society. The Sligo Ribbonmen had already been shaken by the discoveries made by William Faussett in 1836, and so the system in the town had been carried on with the utmost secrecy until 1841.[32]

As far as the extant sources indicate, the first informer to provide evidence on the Ribbon system in Sligo was a Ribbonman named Michael McGarry, who, according to John O'Brien, had been arrested for another incident in the town and had been persuaded to give up his Ribbon membership as a result: 'In the latter end of 1839 an accident put the then county delegate, Mich.l [sic] McGarry in my power, and I availed myself of this to induce him to renounce the society and to give me information, which he did, but he refused to give any that would implicate others, and as I had no charge against him I could not compel him'.[33] Since McGarry would not provide information on particular Ribbon colleagues, the details that O'Brien obtained from him in late 1839 were not of any particular use. However, in the Autumn of 1841, the Sligo authorities were presented with an opportunity which they must have hardly dared to believe possible: on 23 September a tobacco pipe maker in the town complained to the magistrates of a system of combination among the men of that trade in the town which had resulted in that man's son, who was an apprentice to the same trade, having to leave his employment in Sligo and move to another part of the country. The tobacco pipe maker named three men who he knew to be the leaders of the combination among the pipe makers – one of these three men was James Hagan, who the informant also swore was a leading member of the Ribbon society in Sligo town.[34] William Faussett and John O'Brien, the two magistrates before whom the pipe maker swore his informations, already knew that Hagan was the most powerful Ribbonman in Sligo, but up until September 1841 they had been constricted by a lack of evidence in apprehending him. Now, however, they had a substantial charge on which to arrest Hagan and search his premises without giving him any forewarning. James Hagan and the two other men accused of combination among the pipe makers were arrested on or around 23 September 1841 and a search of Hagan's house in Market Street by the constabulary revealed several documents belonging to the Ribbon secret society which provided enough evidence for the magistrates to hold Hagan on the additional charge of Ribbonism.[35] On 25 September, James Hagan summoned the provost, William Faussett, to attend him in Sligo prison. During his interview with Faussett, Hagan admitted to being a member of the Ribbon society in Sligo town and proceeded to give information on the delegate meetings of the Ulster faction – he admitted to being present at the Annayalla meeting in Monaghan in April 1841, and informed the authorities of the details of the upcoming delegate meeting that was due to be held in Middletown, Co. Armagh.[36]

On the strength of Hagan's confession to Faussett, the authorities made arrangements to infiltrate the meeting due to be held at Middletown on 7 October 1841. An undercover policeman attended at Middletown and as a result, six Ribbon delegates were arrested in the meeting room. They were John Brady, Hugh O'Hara, Henry Hughes, John Rice, Patrick O'Hare and Patrick Cavanagh, the delegates for Cavan, Down, Armagh, Monaghan, Glasgow and Liverpool respectively. Due to a lack of evidence, only two of the arrested, John Brady and Hugh O'Hara, were detained for trial, the others were let go free. Rice, Cavanagh and Hughes, were later re-arrested when more evidence was discovered. However, Patrick O'Hare, the Glasgow delegate, escaped.[37] Since he had been imprisoned at the time, and had not yet been known to have given information to the authorities, Hagan had sent his borough master, Daniel Fitzpatrick, to the delegate meeting at Middletown in Armagh. Fitzpatrick had escaped arrest at Middletown, and returned to Hagan in Sligo with the details of the meeting, which the latter provided in turn to the magistrates. Hagan also continued to correspond with the escaped Glasgow delegate, Patrick O'Hare, in an attempt to aid in his apprehension. Hagan was bailed in October 1841 and he attended the next delegate meeting himself which took place at Derrynoose in Co. Armagh on Christmas Day, 1841, after which he brought the information back to the Sligo authorities.[38] However, John O'Brien, the Sligo magistrate, was becoming suspicious of Hagan's information by this stage, and was also unhappy at the manner in which he had apparently evaded the constabulary surveillance placed on him in Derrynoose:

> I have now to state that I think Hagan's present statement is more inconsistent than any formerly made by him. I have little doubt but he intentionally avoided Const. [sic] Johnston who I am certain did his duty faithfully and anxiously and that he Hagan remained secreted lest he should meet the Constable. It is likely that some such meeting as he describes was held at Derrinse [sic].[39]

O'Brien and his magisterial colleagues in Sligo were even more unhappy when they realized in December 1841 the full extent of Hagan's activities in the Ribbon system after he had been bailed the previous October. James Hagan had not alone continued to carry on his delegate duties in the Ribbon society on his release from Sligo prison, but he had also continued to actively recruit new members into the secret society, confident that as an informer his value to the government was too great for them to interfere with his remunerative swearing activities. It was this aspect of his Ribbon activities in Sligo town that was castigated most in the ballad 'The downfall of Hagan' in 1842. For a period of four months from October 1841, Hagan had, it seemed, wilfully sworn young men into an illegal secret society that he had been, at the same time, supplying the government with information on – this was viewed at a popular level in Sligo as particularly duplicitous on Hagan's part, especially as his information would be used to indict local men. He later claimed when questioned about this duplicity in court, that the authorities were aware that he had continued to write out Ribbon passwords for the society in Sligo and swear new men into the organization.[40] However, the government records show that they were not aware that Hagan was still propagating the Ribbon system in Sligo until John O'Brien received information to that effect on 22 January 1842.[41]

In the meantime, Hagan had been consolidating his position as a reliable informer, and the Sligo authorities had been extremely anxious to protect his identity in order to make the best use possible of his information. It had been a master stroke on Hagan's part to include references to the Carrick faction's desire for French aid and arms in his earlier information to the government – this was one of the reasons why William Faussett wished to protect Hagan longer than Dublin Castle were willing to do so. Local and central authorities differed on their perceptions of the Ribbonmen's ability to communicate with a foreign power. Faussett, the Sligo provost, a Protestant and an Orangeman, felt himself and his comrades to be under siege from the Ribbon society who were, in the words of one of his peers, 'picking off the Protestants one by one', and this was reflected in his determination to find out more about the Ribbonmen's threat to communicate with France.[42] Dublin Castle officials, on the other hand, were more removed from the local stage, and so could view the capabilities of the Ribbonmen with a more objective eye. A letter from one of the government's lawyers in January 1842 conveyed this difference in perception at a central government level:

> I differ altogether with Mr Faussett; my opinion been [sic] that there is no mischief likely to ensue from communications between such persons as Hagan and his associates and any foreign state; the mischief and danger as I conceive resulting from the existence of the Ribbon conspiracy, is, as it immediately bears upon society in Ireland, impeding the progress of trade and agriculture, interfering with the administration of justice, and the difficulties thrown in the way of good government by the numerical force support ready and at hand to political agitators. Under such circumstances it would appear to me to be a loss of valuable time and opportunity to wait longer for further information from Hagan.[43]

All of this contributed to an almost palpable sense of frustration on the part of the local authorities in Sligo once they discovered Hagan's double-dealing in February 1842. John O'Brien castigated James Hagan for his

conduct in a communication from himself and William Faussett to the
government in January:

> I therefore think that we cannot expect any further useful results from
> keeping Hagan in his present situation. On the contrary, I believe that
> he has never worked the Ribbon system with so much energy as since
> he came under our protection. I believe he is cognizent (if not the
> abettor) of the principal outrages lately committed in this district and
> I am certain that the longer he continues here the more will the
> country be demoralized. He has given us very extensive information
> but of what use will this be unless he will prosecute the guilty
> parties.[44]

However, by then the authorities in Dublin Castle were anxious to use
Hagan's information in the 1842 summer assizes, believing him to be their
best chance of breaking up a Ribbon system which had proved remarkably
resilient even after the arrests of leading delegates of both the Ulster and
Leinster factions in the summer of 1840. The under-secretary instructed
Faussett and O'Brien to admit Hagan as a crown approver in January 1842
and that 'no pains or expense should be spared' in using him to indict other
leading Ribbonmen throughout the countryside and in Britain.[45]

Unfortunately for Fausset, O'Brien, and the other magistrates in Sligo,
things were yet again about to take a turn for the worse with regard to the
Ribbon society. It had been determined by the authorities in the town that
rather than attempting to arrest all the men that Hagan had named as
Ribbonmen in the town and county of Sligo, which numbered 63 parish
masters alone, they would only arrest five of the leading Ribbonmen in
Sligo town and search their houses. Hagan was to be arrested also in order to
maintain the pretence that he had not yet given information on the system
to the authorities. In fact, it was even decided to plant papers at Hagan's
house deliberately, in order to allow the arresting party to make a sensational
discovery.[46] However, on the morning of Monday, 7 February 1842, the day
that the arrests were to be carried out, James Hagan went to the house of
one of his closest Ribbon comrades in Sligo town, that of his borough
master, Daniel Fitzpatrick, and warned the latter and some other Ribbonmen
present at the time, to leave the town before they were arrested. According
to Fitzpatrick's later information, Hagan had told them 'that he Hagan
intended to leave town, as there were several informations against him, and
that he would advise them to do the same, that on the previous night a
Police Man [sic] called at his house, asked was he there yet, and said that if
he remained longer he would be arrested.' As no policeman or other
authority figure would have had reason to visit Hagan's house before 7
February 1842, the story that Hagan told Fitzpatrick was undoubtedly a false

one, made up either to protect men Hagan regarded as real friends and comrades, or to protect himself from as much damage as possible once his information to the authorities became public knowledge, as it was bound to once he had been admitted as an approver. Hagan's disclosure resulted in Daniel Fitzpatrick visiting his priest, Revd Owen Feeny, who advised him to go to the magistrate, John O'Brien, and confess his involvement in the Ribbon system. Ironically, Fitzpatrick had, according to his own evidence, already given up the Ribbon system in confession to Revd Feeny the previous week, and so he was able to confess his prior involvement to the authorities while stressing that he was no longer part of the illegal Ribbon system.[47] Once the news travelled around the community, other local Ribbon leaders in the town went to the magistrates and confessed that they had been or were then Ribbonmen. For the authorities, the effects of Hagan's actions meant that all the information he had provided them with in regard to Ribbonism in Sligo town was now useless – once the men came to the authorities, admitted to having been members of the Ribbon society in the past, and swore not to be associated with the society in the future, the government could not convict them. In addition to this, the authorities had no hope of locating any incriminating documents in any of the men's houses, as they had had plenty of time to destroy all before making their way to the magistrates. Faussett's anger with this development was almost tangible in the letter he sent informing government of the latest turn of events in the town, in which he blamed Hagan for forewarning the men of the government's intentions:

> [Hagan] induced them to come forward to give *countenance* that he was doing no disclosing of secrets and giving up the system, it had this bad effect, it put them on their guard and prevented papers being found with them – I enclose the statement made by the different *persons.* You will perceive they *only comply* with being Ribbonmen – but refused making any disclosure that would lead to discover their accomplices or upset the system – I regret *exceedingly* that any arrests have been made until a general search and arrest of all the leaders – what has been *done* will make them more cautious, and will have little effect in pulling down a combination of twenty thousand *persons* in this county alone – unless followed up with determination and to show them that the law is too strong for them and must take effect.[48]

Faussett also believed that the interference of the local Catholic clergy, whom the Ribbonmen had claimed had prompted them to confess to the authorities, had been less than helpful, in that it had pre-empted the magistrates' actions.[49] It appeared that on the day before the arrests were due to take place, Revd Feeny had castigated the Ribbonmen from the altar, and this was the motive given by some of the Sligo Ribbonmen when they gave themselves up to the police.[50] John O'Brien, on the other hand, was much more supportive of the clergy's involvement in the process, regarding this as the only way that such a widespread conspiracy as Ribbonism could be put down in the county:

> Their [Roman Catholic clergy] influence with the class of person concerned is greater than any other which could be brought to bear against them. I think it is the best [way] the system can be got rid of and that in other counties the example may be followed... According to Hagan's evidence the number of Ribbonmen in the county amounts to several thousands, admitting ... that account may be greatly exaggerated, and [that] they are from one to two thousand ... [the] Government could not contemplate the prosecution and punishment of such a number, and if only a few are prosecuted... their places will be ... supplied as is proved by the consequences of the trials at Carrick on Shannon and elsewhere.[51]

This aspect of the possible connivance of the local Catholic priest with the Sligo Ribbonmen was to have dire repercussions for John O'Brien, who was himself a Roman Catholic. Allegations were made in the *Limerick Chronicle* in March 1842 that the Ribbonmen in Sligo had been forewarned of the authorities' intentions because O'Brien had divulged secret information to his wife, who in turn had informed her priest, Revd Owen Feeny, of the events.[52] This, according to the paper, was the real reason for the Ribbonmen's preventative actions in Sligo. Revd Feeny vehemently denied the allegation in the *Freeman's Journal* the following week:

> Whether this source from which he [London correspondent of the *Limerick Chronicle*] derives his knowledge, may or may not be authentic, I will not take any trouble to inquire ... But against the injustice of attributing Mr O'Brien's dismissal to me, or any acts of mine, I must loudly protest, having had no communication from or with Mr O'Brien, or any member of his amiable family, either directly or indirectly, on the subject; no, not even the slightest knowledge, when I did speak on that Sunday against illegal societies.[53]

Despite Feeny's denials, O'Brien was removed from his position as magistrate in Sligo, although it appeared that the reasons for his removal were a little more complex than first reported.[54] Whatever the cause for his dismissal from Sligo, the controversy surrounding O'Brien's relationship with the Catholic clergy in the town provides some insights into the difficulties that Catholic magistrates may have experienced in carrying out their duties in the heightened sectarian atmosphere of pre-Famine Ireland. However, despite the interference or otherwise of local clergy in getting Ribbonmen to renounce their membership of the society, it appeared that James Hagan had, unwittingly or otherwise, outsmarted the authorities in Sligo town.

As a result of these events, Hagan was rearrested and remanded in Dublin. He was also forced to testify against former Ribbon colleagues at the 1842 summer assizes in both Armagh and Longford. Hagan was very clear while testifying at the assizes that the only reason for his doing so was the fact that he had been threatened with transportation if he didn't.[55] In fact Hagan made it clear during his evidence in court that he would still be propagating the Ribbon society among his peers if he had not been arrested and furthermore that he maintained an emotional attachment to the Ribbon secret society: 'I was fond of the Ribbon society – some of my pleasantest [sic] hours were spent in it and I love the society still'.[56] It does appear that the authorities had put some amount of pressure on Hagan to prosecute in 1842 – he claimed that he had been imprisoned in Dublin from February to July and had not been treated very well while incarcerated; he also made it clear that he did not receive any money from the authorities.[57] It was reasonable for James Hagan to assume that he would be transported in 1842 if he did not agree to testify at that year's Ribbon trials – both his Cavan and Tyrone Ribbon counterparts had been transported for Ribbonism in 1840.

The first trials that Hagan appeared at as the government's main approver took place at the Armagh assizes in March 1842. The defendants were four Ribbon delegates who were arrested after the delegate meeting that took place at Middletown in Co. Armagh on 7 October 1841. Among the four men were John Rice, the Monaghan county delegate and one of the leading members of the ruling board of the Ulster faction; Hugh O'Hara, the delegate for Co. Down; Patrick Cavanagh, a leading member of the secret society in Liverpool; and Henry Hughes, the Armagh delegate for Ulster Ribbonism.[58] A fifth man, Patrick O'Hare, the Glasgow delegate for Ulster Ribbonism, had also been arrested at Middletown, but had absconded before the trial took place.[59] All were charged with being members of a secret society, unlawful combination and confederacy. Hagan was the first witness put on the stand. He admitted being a member of a society called the Knights of Saint Patrick, or the Order of Liberators, also known as the Ribbonmen. He provided the court with the history of his own membership in the society and also described the signs and passwords used by the association. He then moved on to give evidence on the delegate meeting that he had attended at Middletown in Armagh in October 1841. He identified the four prisoners that were present that day in Middletown as representatives of their various lodges and districts. According to Hagan, he had known some of these men for a number of years before they were arrested – he told of attending delegate meetings in Dundalk and Enniskillen with John Rice, in 1834 and 1838 respectively.

Under examination, Hagan described the various documents for the court which the constabulary had confiscated in both his own, and other Ribbonmen's houses previous to the trials. Among the Ribbon documents produced at the trial were copies of travelling certificates. Hagan gave an account of their use among the Ribbonmen: 'people getting these got work on going to a strange place, and if not they were supported.' When cross-examined, he claimed that he saw no great harm in the Ribbonmen's use of such documents. Some of the other documents produced at the trial included a copy of the rules for delegates of the society and a certificate for swearing new members into the movement. Hagan also identified personal letters that he had received from other members of the society – among these were a number of communications from the parish master of a lodge in Glasgow, Peter Meehan, and a couple of letters from Patrick O'Hare, the delegate for Glasgow.[60] In his evidence, Hagan claimed that he did not know Meehan, the Glasgow parish master, personally, but that he had corresponded with him for the previous eight years, indicating to some extent, the sheer size of the Ribbon society in the 1830s – this was precisely what enabled the authorities to infiltrate the Ulster Ribbon faction in the early 1840s. Representatives of the British Ribbon lodges, whose letters had been intercepted and copied by the government through the post office system, were then impersonated by undercover police officers who were confident that the contacts they would meet in Ireland, in many instances, did not know what some of their English counterparts looked like.[61] Hagan concluded his evidence by identifying the signatures of some of the men on trial.

Before the court Hagan had to defend his unorthodox behaviour after his release from prison in 1841. His stout defence of his character under interrogation gave some insight into his perception of his own identity, 'I am a tradesman, a tobacco pipe manufacturer; I am a Sligo man and a Roman Catholic of course'. He admitted attending Ribbon meetings and carrying on with the business of the secret society after his release on bail in 1841, for which he claimed he provided heavy security, and he even went so far as to imply that he would still be attending the Ribbon meetings if he could, claiming, 'it is not my fault that I am not'.[62] But he also denied that he would rejoin the society if he was liberated again. Hagan claimed in his evidence that the police and magistrates knew that he was still attending the business of the society after his release, but that they did not tell him to do so. After Hagan's cross-examination, Timothy Cox, a sub-constable, who attended the Ribbon meeting in Middletown in plain clothes, gave evidence against the prisoners. He was followed on the stand by William Mathew, a sub-inspector of constabulary in Co. Monaghan, who led the police party that raided the Middletown meeting. Mathew claimed that the prisoners were discovered in an inner room upstairs in a public house and that some of the documents produced at the trial had been discovered in the room with them. Following Mathew's evidence, the defence lawyer, Mr Tomb, objected to the inclusion of Hagan's version of the Ribbon passwords as evidence against the prisoners; he claimed that that particular copy of the passwords had been written by Hagan in his own house in Sligo town at a much earlier date than those words found in the possession of the prisoners. The attorney general pointed out that the passwords were exact copies of those found in the home of John Rice in Monaghan, and as such, they corroborated Hagan's evidence. Tomb then addressed the jury at length, but called no witnesses for the defence. The jury were then locked up for the night as the trial had lasted from the morning time. When the assizes recommenced the next morning, they still had not agreed on a verdict and were discharged by the judge. The five prisoners were released on bail to be retried at the summer assizes.[63]

The next trial to come before the Armagh assizes was that of James McCone, who was charged with being a member of 'a certain unlawful society' at Derrynoose in Co. Armagh. James Hagan was also the crown's primary witness in this case. He claimed that he had seen McCone at Derrynoose and that he had also met him at previous delegate meetings in Dundalk and Enniskillen. Hagan was again cross-examined by Tomb, this time on whether he understood the nature and obligation of an oath, the implication being that as he had broken his Ribbon oaths, there was nothing to prevent him lying to the courts also. Again, Hagan defended himself vigorously in the face of Tomb's accusations. The same members of the constabulary were called to corroborate the Ribbon documents produced at McCone's trial, as had been called at the previous day's proceedings. No new evidence was produced, and again, no witnesses were called for the defence. The jury retired once the evidence was completed, and once again, they could not agree on a verdict. According to the report of the trials in the *Sligo Journal*, the reason for the lack of convictions in both trials was clear: 'all the Roman Catholics in both, we understand, holding out against a conviction. There were ten Protestants and two Roman Catholics on the Jury'.[64]

The next trial at which Hagan provided evidence for the crown against the Ribbonmen was at the Longford summer assizes in July 1842. The defendant was Francis M'Canna, a leading member of the Ribbon society in Co. Longford. The information that Hagan provided against M'Canna was largely a repetition of what he had claimed in the previous trials at Armagh in March. However, it appeared that M'Canna made some attempt to defend himself at his trial and Hagan was challenged as to how he knew the details of the Middletown meeting. The latter replied that he had been in jail when the Middletown meeting had taken place, but that he had gotten the reports of the proceedings from the Sligo borough master who had gone to the meeting in place of the county delegate. During the trial, Hagan had identified the handwriting in a copybook found in M'Canna's house as being a copy of the relevant quarter's passwords for the Ribbon society. When questioned by the court as to how he could be so sure about the origins of those words, Hagan elaborated further on how the Ribbon passwords circulated around the countryside:

> The way I know that the passwords written in the copybook were given out at the Middletown meeting is, that they were given to me by my parish master, and afterwards sent to the county of Longford. Every member of the society who is not in debt is entitled to a certificate, which is of use only for three months, and since I gave out the October passwords to Longford, more than fifty persons have come to me from different parts of the county with their certificates, which were word for word the same as the October passwords I have repeated.[65]

Hagan's defence of his testimony and his careful explanation of the workings of the secret society in Co. Longford obviously affected the jury. They deliberated for only a short while before finding Francis M'Canna guilty and he was sentenced to seven years transportation, a heavy penalty indeed given that some of the Ribbon delegates arrested in Ballinamore, Co. Leitrim in 1840 had only received two years imprisonment.[66]

James Hagan was kept as an approver in the bridewell at Richmond in Dublin between the spring and summer assizes of 1842.[67] His evidence was to be used again in the retrial of the Armagh delegates later in the year. The second trial of the original four defendants, John Rice, Hugh O'Hara, Patrick Cavanagh and Henry Hughes was arranged to take place on 22 July 1842. Patrick O'Hare, the Glasgow delegate, had still not been arrested. On the day of the trial, Patrick Cavanagh, the Liverpool delegate, did not turn up and his recognizances were duly estreated. A sixth man, John Brady, who had been arrested at the Middletown Ribbon meeting, was also tried on this occasion.[68] The evidence produced during the second trial was largely the same as that produced during the original hearing. There was, however, a much greater stress on the importance of Hagan's role as an approver and the attorney general addressed this issue at length in his opening statements to the court. While acknowledging that Hagan was an informer, he was keen to stress the cool and deliberate manner in which the approver gave his evidence, thereby indicating that there was some unease in the public arena over Hagan's role as a crown approver in the trials against the Ribbonmen:

The learned counsel then stated some evidence relative to two of the prisoners, which he said was chiefly important as bearing on the testimony of a man who would appear before them. His name was Hagan, and true it is, he is an informer, but you will find him corroborated in his evidence; and if he give it as he did before, no man could give his testimony in a more clear, satisfactory way ... Having since seen him on that table, and observed his unimpassioned tone, if it be now as it were at the last assizes, I would appeal to you whether it does not impress you with the feeling of the truth and accuracy of his statement, and if he be not gifted with the spirit of prophecy, it appears impossible he could foretell in the manner in which he did predict a meeting which took place of this society, of which you shall hear.[69]

The attorney general's desire to maintain Hagan's credibility as an approver was directly linked to the debate that had begun in the public arena over the propriety of the crown's use of James Hagan as an informer against the Ribbonmen. This debate centred around the evidence that Hagan had given at the spring assizes in Armagh where he had maintained that he had been very active in swearing-in new members to the Ribbon society while he had been giving information to the authorities in Sligo, and that the magistrates had been aware of his activities.[70] The attorney general's statements at the end of July were an attempt to answer the questions surrounding the use of this particular approver. However, on 1 August both Richard Shiel and Daniel O'Connell raised the matter in the house of commons, inquiring of the government whether they had played a role in the entrapment of members of the Ribbon society in Ireland.[71] William Faussett strenuously denied the allegations made by Shiel in parliament in a letter to Dublin Castle in August 1842, 'The charge made by Mr Shiel in the House of Commons ... is totally unfounded – as both Mr O'Brien and I cautioned him [Hagan] against such proceedings.'[72] Hagan himself was very careful in his evidence during the second trial in Armagh to set the record straight for the government, directly contradicting some of his earlier public statements, 'after I was let out the police had no more notion of what I was at in the society than you [sic] had; I had an opportunity then to make Ribbonmen by the hundred, I concocted about sixty-six Ribbon documents when out of gaol'.[73] He further refuted any claims that he might have been benefiting financially from his current actions, maintaining that his present existence was not one that he would have chosen if he had had any other option,

My former business, a pipemaker, was a very good one, better than my present one, I would prefer to carry stones all the days of my life, in a creel upon my back, than be an informer; nothing but being twice sworn against by members of the society made me an informer.[74]

Despite any public misgivings about the use of James Hagan as an informer in the trials of the four Ribbonmen, the jury did not take long to return a verdict of guilty for all four of them. James McCone, the Armagh Ribbonman who had been tried separately to the original five delegates at the Armagh spring assizes and had also been released when the jury had not agreed, was retried at the county's summer assizes the day after the major trial as he had been in March 1842. Most likely because of the success of Hagan's testimony on the previous day, McCone did not offer any defence this time around and pleaded guilty to the offence he was charged with. Again, the attorney general took the stand to defend the crown from allegations made by Tomb, the defence counsel, that Hagan had been used to entrap innocent men into committing crimes for which they were now about to be punished. The presiding judge, Crampton, then stated that he hoped all members of the Ribbon society would take heed of the example about to be set them, indicating that the sentences would not be light. All four delegates from the first trial and James McCone were sentenced to seven years transportation. This was the end of James Hagan's role as a crown approver against the Ribbonmen, and as the *Sligo Journal* sombrely noted at the end of its coverage of that summer's events, 'Thus ended, to this part of the Kingdom in particular, these important trials.'[75]

Conclusion

The career of James Hagan, the Sligo county Ribbon delegate, is not an easy one to follow. What the historian is left with is a snapshot of a life viewed through the lens of police reports, magistrates' letters and the published accounts of assizes. Before Hagan was arrested in September 1841, his was just one name in a list of Sligo Ribbonmen provided by earlier informers in the 1830s. Similarly, once Hagan had finished giving information on behalf of the crown at the 1842 assizes, details on him in the official sources once more dry up. It is probable that James and Catherine Hagan and their family were given funds to emigrate for their own protection after the events of 1841–2. Not surprisingly, the circulation and apparent popularity of the ballad 'The downfall of Hagan' in Sligo town in 1842 suggests that the approver was deeply unpopular in his hometown and the public furore over his possible entrapment of Ribbonmen would only have added to his notoriety throughout that part of the country. In addition, his role in transporting 21 year-old Francis M'Canna from Longford along with the county delegates of Monaghan, Armagh and Down ensured that there were few places in Ireland, or indeed Irish centres in Britain, in which Hagan could have safely resided by the end of the summer of 1842.[1] Along with this, Hagan's economic existence as a tobacco pipe maker was sufficiently low among the petty trading strata of Sligo town to ensure that no commercial records exist for him in the form of trade directory entries or newspaper advertisements.

However, the information of James Hagan and others not only exposed the sheer extent of the activities of the Ribbon secret society in Sligo and elsewhere, it also provided insights into an intricate web of social and economic networking controlled by the secret society among the lower trading strata of Sligo town and county and the extension of those networks into the surrounding counties of Leitrim, Roscommon and Longford. Hagan's initial arrest was for organizing a trade combination among the pipe makers of Sligo town, a combination that had forced at least one young apprentice out of the town to find work elsewhere. The carmen in Sligo and the surrounding counties were also under pressure to purchase the relevant Ribbon passwords in order to ensure the safe passage of their goods from local markets and fairs. Local traders purchased the passwords for the same reason while at the same time trying to stay within the confines of the law by not swearing the Ribbon oath. Through these mechanisms, the

Ribbonmen's passwords were a commodity that controlled local petty trading and transport networks. Tom Garvin has noted how the protectionist trading policies propagated by the Ribbonmen were often simply a mask for an organized protection racket, and the Ribbonmen in Sligo were in many ways a perfect example of this type of economic monopoly.[2] Failure to comply with the informal trading and transport routes controlled by the Ribbon society led to intimidation and reprisal for petty traders and artisans. In this way, men who were not members of a local Ribbon lodge often found themselves subject to its strictures, ensuring that the Ribbon society had an influence on the local trading community that far outstretched the boundaries of the lodges.

On the other hand, all the evidence suggests that the early-19th century Ribbon lodge in Co. Sligo did not have any problems extending its influence throughout the surrounding countryside. The lodge provided an important social as well as economic status for men in local parishes throughout the county. Along with benefiting their economic existence in the form of enforcing protectionist policies in local fairs and markets, the complex lines of internal hierarchies within the Ribbon society, encompassing distinct rural and urban lines of command, provided a social pecking order for men who, by virtue of their social status, lived among the lower ranks of a wider political society. Progression through the Ribbonite hierarchy to parish master, borough master or even county delegate level also provided opportunities to enhance the economic status of the individual member. In addition, for those who never made it to the governing levels of the society, accession to the regular body of Ribbonmen still admitted them to an electable elite within the secret society from which a lower order of Ribbonman, the three-penny-man, was excluded. In fact, the existence of three-penny-men in Sligo poses further questions about the nature of the overlap that existed between the Ribbon society proper and the ubiquitous semi-autonomous agrarian gangs that traversed the rural countryside in the early 19th century. The sources for Sligo Ribbonism also provide insights into the manner in which the secret society functioned within the wider society in which it operated. Ribbon involvement in local trade combinations and also in local political events such as the 1837 borough election suggest that the objectives of the Ribbonmen were sometimes indistinguishable from wider community popular practice, but at the same time this should not be taken to imply that the *raison d'etre* of Ribbonism was necessarily the protection of local communities from external threats posed by an increasingly centralized political system and an ever-encroaching market economy. The Ribbonmen in Co. Sligo did not pay their quarterly subscription dues to benefit their local communities, but in order to augment their own position in their local parishes or townlands.

James Hagan's career as a Ribbonman is a prime example of the type of opportunities available to men of his class on joining the society. He joined the society as a young apprentice in the mid-1820s, and 11 years later he occupied the most powerful Ribbon position in Sligo town, that of the county delegate. His progression through the ranks of the society had afforded him an influence among his peers, both at a social and economic level, that might not otherwise have been possible for him to achieve. As county delegate he managed and arbitrated the disputes of all of the other members in the county, and more importantly, he controlled access to the coveted Ribbon passwords and other communications that came from the ruling board of the Ulster faction of Ribbonism. However, his progression to the top of the local Ribbonite hierarchy was not uncontested; in 1836 he was not the first choice candidate to accede to the county delegate's position and it is clear that some amount of negotiations were conducted in order for him to be given the position. In fact there may even have been a physical force element to his accession to the leadership of the society in the county. This type of challenge for positions of prominence within the society's hierarchy was a feature of the Ribbon society generally in the early 19th century and Hagan was not the only delegate who had to fight to maintain his position in the society. Once elected as county delegate, however, Hagan consolidated his power within the society further – from 1840 on he was a member of a select group within the Ulster faction and privy to the innermost workings of the Ribbon system. This was why Hagan's capture in September 1841 was such a coup for the Sligo authorities.

Of course, there were other reasons besides a desire for economic advancement for joining the Ribbon society in the early 19th century. Not least among these were the camaraderie and real friendships that existed among members who knew each other for years through their participation in the Ribbon system. For those members at the top of the Ribbonite hierarchy, such friendships existed over long regional distances, even crossing the Irish Sea in some cases. In Hagan's case he had met with the men he prosecuted many times over the course of several years, each meeting involving at least some amount of conviviality in the form of sharing meals and heavy drinking. Other contacts that he had maintained through his practice of Ribbonism were not quite personal friendships but were no less well maintained for that – Hagan's correspondence with Peter Meehan in Glasgow, a man that he had never met, was conducted regularly over a period of some eight years. On a local level in Sligo town, the evidence suggests that the men who conducted the lodges in the town were friends with each other. Certainly Hagan's relationship with Daniel Fitzpatrick, who was his second-in-command in the town, suggested a certain amount of trust between the two men, and it is tempting to assume that Hagan's warning to Fitzpatrick of his impending arrest in 1842 was more an attempt to save a good friend from prosecution and possible transportation, than a desire to save his own skin. Hagan's description of his membership of the Ribbon society as some of the 'pleasantest hours' he had ever spent adds further colour to a picture of the society as a source of recreation and fun for its members.

Once James Hagan was arrested in the autumn of 1841, he must have known that he was in a particularly difficult position. He had been known to the authorities as a senior Ribbonman in the town since at least 1836, and now they had enough evidence to convict him not just of membership of an illegal society, but of involvement in local combinations also. His subsequent decision to turn informer against his former associates was an obvious attempt to save himself from prosecution. However, the manner in which he managed his position as informer – feeding the authorities all the information they required, while at the same time working harder than ever to increase the Ribbon system in Sligo – marked him out for particular odium by both the local magistrates and the wider community in the town. For the government, James Hagan proved to be a particularly successful informer and this was one of the main reasons why the allegation of entrapment was made after the Armagh trials in 1842. In general, informers were notoriously unreliable and convictions could not be guaranteed without corroborating evidence. Hagan was, though, a reliable witness for the Crown; he was consistent and articulate in the way he provided his evidence and he was also able to refute the attacks made on his character by the defence counsel.

Many questions will remain about James Hagan, the Sligo Ribbonman. Some of them may be answered by further study. Among those that will probably never be resolved are why he acted as he did when released on bail in October 1841 – did he increase his swearing-in of new Ribbonmen in the county in order to allay any suspicions on the part of his Ribbon comrades that he might have informed? Or was it because he was so confident he could play his involvement in Ribbonism off against the authorities' desire to maintain him as an informer? Did he inform other Sligo Ribbonmen of their impending arrest because he wanted to protect his friends or was he simply attempting to carry on the pretence that he was in as much danger of discovery as they were? Whatever the motivations for his actions, 'The downfall of Hagan' may only have been sung in Sligo town in 1842, but the sentiment behind the ballad must surely have reverberated through the rest of the county as well as in the courtrooms of Longford and Armagh and perhaps even as far afield as the house of commons in London.

Notes

ABBREVIATIONS

NAI   National Archives of Ireland
CSORP, OR   Chief Secretary's Office Registered Papers, Outrage Reports
TNA, PRO: CO   The National Archives of England and Wales, Public Record Office:
                Colonial Office
SJ   *Sligo Journal*
RLG   *Roscommon & Leitrim Gazette*
SC   *Sligo Champion*
FJ   *Freeman's Journal*

1. 'THE DOWNFALL OF HAGAN'

1 NAI, CSORP, OR: attached to 10833 26 1842.
2 NAI, CSORP, OR: 10833 26 1842; 5709 26 1842.
3 NAI, CSORP, OR: 10833 26 1842.
4 TNA, PRO: CO 904/8, ff 393–6.
5 *SJ*, 25 Mar. 1842 & 15 July 1842.
6 NAI, CSORP, OR: 10833 26 1842.
7 NAI, CSORP, OR: 5709 26 1842.
8 See, for example, the information of Michael Navin of Castle Street & that of Michael McGarry, TNA, PRO: CO 904/8, ff 325–6.
9 TNA, PRO: CO 904/9, ff 120–1.
10 NAI, CSORP, OR: 10833 26 1842.
11 TNA, PRO: CO 904/9, ff 33–5.
12 NAI, CSORP, OR: 10833 26 1842
13 See, for example, Justice Ball's comments on the conviction of Richard Jones for membership of the Leinster faction of Ribbonism in 1840: *RLG*, 4 July 1840.
14 Maura Murphy, 'The ballad singer and the role of the seditious ballad in nineteenth-century Ireland: Dublin Castle's view', in *Ulster Folklife*, 25 (1979), 96.
15 NAI, CSORP, OR: attached to 10833 26 1842.
16 NAI, CSORP, OR: 10833 26 1842.

17 TNA, PRO: CO 904/9, ff 120–1. Hagan stated that between 1825 and 1831, he alone swore 2,000 men into the Ribbon society in Sligo: *SJ*, 15 July 1842.

2. THE RIBBON SOCIETY IN SLIGO

1 *SJ*, 15 July 1842.
2 TNA, PRO: CO 904/7, ff 345–347 & CO 904/8, ff 326–7.
3 A letter from a ruling member of the Leinster Ribbon faction complained of the paucity of members in Sligo and other regions: 'If any of your members are going on tramp you can supply them with a certificate, by which means they will be received in the following places by those persons who act as presidents … Leitrim Captain Fitzpatrick and Farrell Curran Ballinamore … We do not know of any being in the following counties Clare, Kerry, Limerick, Cork, Waterford, Kilkenny, Wexford, Galway, Sligo and Mayo', NAI, Kemmis Papers, Frazer MSS, no. 43, 'Transcript of the books written in shorthand found on the person of Richard Jones on 01/10/1839' (hereafter cited as Jones' letters), letter no. 96.

4 NAI, CSORP, Private Papers, 1836, 277 4.

5 Knox's Street was the main street in the town; the name was changed to O'Connell Street in 1898. See John C. McTernan, *In Sligo long ago: aspects of town and county over two centuries* (Sligo, 1998), p. 515.

6 There is no James Campbell mentioned in Sligo town in either Pigot's 1824 directory or Slater's 1846 directory.

7 *Pigot's Directory of Ireland* (Dublin, 1824), p. 216.

8 NAI, CSORP, Private Papers, 1836, 277 4.

9 TNA, PRO: CO 904/9, ff 218–19: The ten men named by James Hagan as body masters in Sligo town were Peter Conway, Henry Hudson, Henry Mulligan, Michael Gaffney, John Cunningham, John Gillan, Patrick Fadden, Denis Keighran, Daniel Fitzpatrick and Bartly Cunningham.

10 NAI, CSORP, Private Papers, 1836, 277 4.

11 NAI, CSORP, OR: 37 26 1836.

12 NAI, CSORP, OR: 78 26 1836.

13 TNA, PRO: CO 904/7, f 114.

14 NAI, CSORP, OR: 13555 26 1840.

15 TNA, PRO: CO 904/9, ff 218–19.

16 Evidence of William S. Tracy Esq., *Report from the Select Committee of the House of Lords appointed to enquire into the state of Ireland in respect of crime*, BPP, 1839 [486], i, p. 371.

17 *SJ*, 25 Mar. 1842; CSORP, Private Papers, 1836, 277 4.

18 *RLG*, 16 July 1842.

19 Ibid. The information that Hagan gave to the magistrates included the names of all the parish and body masters in Sligo town and county, and also included names of Ribbonmen from north Leitrim: TNA, PRO: CO 904/9, ff 218–19.

20 R.V. Comerford, *The Fenians in context: Irish politics & society, 1848–82* (Dublin, 1998), p. 124.

21 Evidence of William Faussett Esq., *Select Committee on crime*, p. 206.

22 Ibid., p. 206.

23 M.R. Beames, 'The Ribbon societies: lower-class nationalism in pre-Famine Ireland,' in C.H.E. Philpin (ed.) *Nationalism & popular protest in Ireland* (Cambridge, 2002), pp 247–9; Tom Garvin, 'Defenders, Ribbonmen & others: underground political networks in pre-Famine Ireland,' in Philpin (ed.) *Nationalism & popular protest in Ireland*, pp 240–2; A.C. Murray, 'Agrarian violence and nationalism in nineteenth century Ireland: the myth of Ribbonism', in *Irish Economic & Social History*, 13 (1986), p. 67; Jennifer Kelly, 'An outward looking community?: Ribbonism & popular mobilization in Co. Leitrim 1836–1846', [hereinafter cited as 'Ribbonism & popular mobilization'] (Unpublished PhD thesis, Mary Immaculate College, University of Limerick, 2005), pp 113–55.

24 NAI, CSORP, Private Papers, 1836, 277.

25 See the comments of the presiding judge, Justice Ball, and the Attorney General at the trial of the Ribbonman, Richard Jones, in 1840 for more on contemporary social perceptions of the Ribbonmen: *RLG*, 4 July 1840.

26 TNA, PRO: CO 904/8, ff 393–6; *SC*, 23 July 1842.

27 NAI, CSORP, Private Papers, 1836, 1705.

28 NAI, CSORP, Private Papers, 1836, 277 4.

29 Ibid.

30 Evidence of William Faussett Esq., *Select Committee on crime*, p. 201.

31 TNA, PRO: CO 904/8, f. 407 & f. 443.

32 Kelly, 'Ribbonism & popular mobilization', pp 128–9.

33 The leaders of Sligo town lodges in 1842 were described by the Stipendiary Magistrate, John O'Brien as body masters: TNA, PRO: CO 904/9, ff 120–1. On the other hand, James Hagan identified one of the men that O'Brien alluded to as being just under him in office in Sligo town and he called him a parish master: *SJ*, 25 Mar. 1842.

34 TNA, PRO: CO 904/8, ff 326–7.

35 TNA, PRO: CO 904/7, f. 188.

36 TNA, PRO: CO 904/9, ff 10–12.
37 See, for example, the evidence of James Monaghan, NAI, CSORP, Private Papers, 1836, 277 4.
38 TNA, PRO: CO 904/8, ff 326–7.
39 A letter from a rural Ribbon lodge in Dromahair in north Leitrim alluded to a set of 'Guardians' or senior members who were unhappy with the conduct of their parish master, indicating that this lodge had a relatively developed structure of internal command: NAI, Kemmis Papers, Frazer MSS, no. 44: 'Reports of the several trials of members of the Ribbon Society on the North West, North East & Connaught Circuits at Summer Assizes 1840.' In other instances, however, local Ribbon lodge membership appeared to be less structured, with members not necessarily aware of a command structure other than that of their immediate leader: NAI, CSORP, OR: 3111 4 1839.
40 TNA, PRO: CO 904/8, ff 155–62; 904/9, ff 10–12.
41 *RLG*, 5 Mar. 1842.
42 Kelly, 'Ribbonism & popular mobilization,' pp 128–31.
43 TNA, PRO: CO 904/8, f. 326 & f. 372.
44 *SJ*, 25 Mar. 1842.
45 Ibid.
46 TNA, PRO: CO 904/7, f. 200 & 904/8, f. 181.
47 Kelly, 'Ribbonism & popular mobilization', pp 114–55.
48 Some Ribbonmen participated in the elections for the local Poor Law Boards in the later 1830s. According to Virginia Crossman, the Poor Law Boards were 'the only administrative body in rural areas with directly elected representatives and as such provided a rare platform from which individuals from the Catholic middle classes could acquire local prominence and influence.' See Virginia Crossman, *Local government in nineteenth-century Ireland* (Belfast, 1994), pp 46 & 53.
49 NAI, Kemmis Papers, Frazer MSS, Reports of trials. See also the *SJ*, 25 Mar. 1842.
50 Kelly, 'Ribbonism & popular mobilization.'
51 Ibid.
52 Evidence of William Faussett Esq., *Select Committee on crime*, p. 199.
53 TNA, PRO: CO 904/8, f. 186.
54 Evidence of William Faussett Esq., *Select Committee on crime*, p. 199.
55 Ibid., p. 194.
56 Evidence of William S. Tracy Esq., *Select Committee on crime*, p. 371.
57 Kelly, 'Ribbonism & popular mobilization', pp 157–203; John Belchem, 'Ribbonism, nationalism & the Irish pub,' in idem, *Merseypride: essays in Liverpool exceptionalism* (Liverpool, 2000), p. 72. According to Belchem, Ribbonism provided 'cheap, flexible and mobile benefits' for Irish migrant labourers in Britain.
58 NAI, Kemmis Papers, Frazer MSS, 'Transcript of the books written in shorthand found on the person of Richard Jones on the 1st of October 1839 – the accounts of the Society in the old book.'
59 Evidence of William Faussett Esq., *Select Committee on crime*, p. 194.
60 TNA, PRO: CO 904/8, ff 155–62.
61 Evidence of William Faussett Esq., *Select Committee on crime*, p. 199.
62 *RLG*, 18 July 1840.
63 *RLG*, 5 Mar. 1842.
64 Kelly, 'Ribbonism & popular mobilization,' p. 148.
65 NAI, CSORP, Private Papers, 1836, 277.
66 Evidence of William Faussett Esq., *Select Committee on crime*, p. 201.
67 NAI, CSORP, OR 21891 16 1842.
68 NAI, Kemmis Papers, Frazer MSS, 'Transcript of the books written in shorthand found on the person of Richard Jones on the 1st of October 1839,' no. 163.
69 NAI, CSORP, OR: 206 16 1839.
70 Kelly, 'Ribbonism & popular mobilization', pp 94–8.
71 Terence Dooley, *The murders at Wildgoose Lodge: agrarian crime and punishment in pre-Famine Ireland* (Dublin, 2007).
72 NAI, CSORP, OR: attached to 206 16 1839.
73 McTernan, *In Sligo long ago*, pp 130–41.
74 NAI, CSORP, OR: 125 26 1837.

75 Evidence of William Faussett Esq.,
    Select Committee on crime, pp 203–4.
76 Ibid., p. 215.
77 NAI, CSORP, OR: 206 16 1839.
78 Evidence of William Faussett Esq.,
    Select Committee on crime, p. 226.
79 *SJ*, 11 Mar. 1836: Some of the
    questions put by the attackers to the
    carman were 'what kind of night it
    was? … what was the ground he
    stood on, that air he breathed, was he
    up to the times, had he anything fresh
    about him &c'.
80 TNA, PRO: CO 904/8, ff 88–9.
81 *SC*, 23 July 1842.
82 See Meehan's information and also
    the attached commentaries by the
    constabulary authorities and the
    Crown Solicitor: NAI, CSORP, OR:
    206 16 1839.
83 TNA, PRO: CO 904/8, f. 325.
84 Ibid.
85 *SC*, 23 July 1842.
86 NAI, CSORP, OR: 14985 26 1842.
87 NAI, CSORP, OR: 14989 26 1842.
88 Evidence of William Faussett Esq.,
    Select Committee on crime, pp 224–6.
89 Ibid., p. 225.

3. JAMES HAGAN: SLIGO RIBBONMAN

1 *SJ*, 04 Mar. 1836 & 25 Mar. 1836.
2 Tom Garvin traced the Ribbon
   society as far back as 1811 in
   informers' reports to Dublin Castle
   where it was described as 'a new term
   for U. Irishmen.' Garvin, 'Defenders,
   Ribbonmen & others', n. 23, p. 232.
3 NAI, CSORP, Private Papers, 1836,
   277 & 277 4.
4 *SJ*, 4 Mar. 1836.
5 NAI, CSORP, Private Papers, 1836,
   277.
6 Ibid.
7 NAI, CSORP, Private Papers, 1836,
   277 4.
8 McTernan, *In Sligo long ago*, pp 530–1.
9 See NAI, CSORP, Private Papers,
   1836, 277 & 277 4 and Faussett's
   evidence before the 1839 committee
   on crime in Ireland for copies of the
   communication carried on between
   James Monaghan and William Faussett.

10 *SJ*, 25 Mar. 1842; NAI, CSORP,
    Private Papers, 1836, 277 4.
11 TNA, PRO: CO 904/9, ff 224–33.
12 NAI, CSORP, Private Papers, 277.
13 Ibid.
14 *SJ*, 25 Mar. 1842.
15 TNA, PRO: CO 904/8, ff 325 & 326.
16 TNA, PRO: CO 904/8, f. 407; *SJ*, 25
    Mar. 1842.
17 Kelly, 'Ribbonism & popular
    mobilization', pp 142–3.
18 TNA, PRO: CO 904/8, f. 407.
19 *SJ*, 25 Mar. 1842.
20 TNA, PRO: CO 904/8, ff 155–62;
    CO 904/8, ff 299–308; RLG, 17 Apr.
    1841.
21 RLG, 13 June 1840.
22 TNA, PRO: CO 904/8, f. 225.
23 Ibid.
24 Ibid.
25 TNA, PRO: CO 904/8, ff 316–17.
26 TNA, PRO: CO 904/9, ff 36–7.
27 See TNA, PRO: CO 904/9, f. 39 for
    evidence of communication between
    James Hagan and the Glasgow
    Ribbon delegate, Patrick O'Hare.
28 TNA, PRO: CO 904/8, ff 155–62.
29 TNA, PRO: CO 904/9, ff 19–21.
30 NAI, CSORP, OR: 13555 26 1840.
31 Ibid.
32 Evidence of William Faussett Esq.,
    Select Committee on crime, p. 200.
33 TNA, PRO: CO 904/8, ff 393–6.
34 TNA, PRO: CO 904/9, ff 191–4.
35 TNA, PRO: CO 904/8, f. 326 & f.
    372. See also TNA, PRO: CO 904/9,
    ff 191–4.
36 TNA, PRO: CO 904/8, ff 369–70 &
    904/9, ff 191–4.
37 TNA, PRO: CO 904/9, ff 191–4.
38 Ibid.
39 TNA, PRO: CO 904/9, ff 10–12.
40 *SJ*, 25 Mar. 1842.
41 TNA, PRO: CO 904/8, ff 336–7: This
    source dates O'Brien's discovery of
    Hagan's activities to 22 February 1842,
    but communications between
    O'Brien and the government on the
    subject are dated 22 January 1842. See
    TNA, PRO: CO 904/9, ff 33–5.
42 The phrase 'picking off the Protestants
    one by one' was attributed to Sir
    William Parke, a Deputy Lieutenant of

Co. Sligo. Evidence of William Faussett Esq., *Select Committee on crime*, p. 216.

43 TNA, PRO: CO 904/9, f. 24: Extract from a letter from W. Hamilton, Sackville Street to Undersecretary Lucas, 10 Jan. 1842.

44 TNA, PRO: CO 904/9, ff 33–5.

45 TNA, PRO: CO 904/9, ff 191–4.

46 Ibid.

47 TNA, PRO: CO 904/9, ff 176–7.

48 TNA, PRO: CO 904/9, ff 117–19.

49 Ibid.

50 *FJ*, 4 Mar. 1842.

51 TNA, PRO: CO 904/9, ff 120–21.

52 The report of the *Limerick Chronicle* was cited in *FJ*, 4 Mar. 1842.

53 *FJ*, 8 Mar. 1842.

54 It appeared that secret information regarding the upcoming Ribbon trials was leaked from O'Brien's office, but the source of the leak was more likely the amanuensis that the magistrate hired to aid him with his voluminous paperwork. *FJ*, 12 Mar. 1842.

55 *SJ*, 25 Mar. 1842.

56 TNA, PRO: CO 904/9, ff 224–33.

57 Ibid.

58 Ibid; TNA, PRO: CO 904/9, ff 189–94.

59 TNA, PRO: CO 904/9, ff 197–202.

60 *SJ*, 25 Mar. 1842; TNA, PRO: CO 904/9, ff 189–94.

61 See, for example, the evidence of Inspector James Mullins, who infiltrated the Ballinamore delegate meeting in 1840 by posing as a new delegate for the Liverpool lodges: TNA, PRO: CO 904/8, ff 155–62.

62 *SJ*, 25 Mar. 1842.

63 Ibid.

64 Ibid.

65 *SJ*, 15 July 1842.

66 Ibid.

67 *SJ*, 29 July 1842.

68 Ibid.

69 Ibid.

70 *SJ*, 25 Mar. 1842.

71 *The Times*, 2 Aug. 1842.

72 TNA, PRO: CO 904/9, f. 231.

73 *SJ*, 29 July 1842.

74 Ibid.

75 Ibid.

CONCLUSION

1 NAI: Ireland–Australia transportation database, http://www.nationalarchives.ie/search/index.php?category=18&advanced=true (9 Jan. 2008).

2 Tom Garvin, *The evolution of Irish nationalist politics* (Dublin, 2005), p. 46.